JUST BECAUSE
I'M LATIN DOESN'T
MEAN I *Mambo*

JUST BECAUSE I'M LATIN DOESN'T MEAN I *M*AMBO

A Success Guide for Hispanic Americans

JUAN ROBERTO JOB

ONE WORLD
THE BALLANTINE PUBLISHING GROUP
NEW YORK

A One World Book
Published by The Ballantine Publishing Group

Copyright © 1998 by Juan Roberto Job

All rights reserved under International
and Pan-American Copyright Conventions. Published
in the United States by The Ballantine Publishing Group, a division
of Random House, Inc., New York, and simultaneously in
Canada by Random House of Canada Limited, Toronto.

http://www.randomhouse.com

LIBRARY OF CONGRESS CATALOGING-IN-PUBLICATION DATA
Job, Juan Roberto.
    Just because I'm Latin doesn't mean I mambo : a success guide for
Hispanic Americans / Juan Roberto Job.
        p.   cm.
    ISBN 0-345-41673-2 (hardcover)
    1. Success in business—United States.   2. Hispanic American
businesspeople.   3. Hispanic American business enterprises—
Management.   I. Title.
HF5386.J58   1998
650.1'0896073—DC21   97-37666
                                                            CIP

Text design by Holly Johnson

Manufactured in the United States of America

First Edition: March 1998

10   9   8   7   6   5   4   3   2   1

Papá Juan
    Mamita
        Papá Angelo
            Tío Domingo
                Honor the legacy
Domínica Luz
    Adrián David
        Maritza Carmen
                Pursue the dream

CONTENTS

CONTENTS

ACKNOWLEDGMENTS

I would like to thank all the dedicated and talented Hispanic professionals who cared enough to share with me their lives, experiences,
successes, challenges, frustrations, advice, anecdotes, sources, information, and good sense. Their values and commitment to others are
inspiring. Although all their names are not written here, I am
nonetheless deeply indebted and forever touched by their contributions and thankful to God for allowing me to be one with them.

I would also like to thank the National Society of Hispanic
MBAs, especially the New York Chapter, the National Hispanic
Employee Association, and the many Hispanic employee associations and organizations for their valuable contributions to this project. In addition, I acknowledge the United States Hispanic Chamber
of Commerce. Their Sixteenth Annual Conference showed me that
they truly "mean business."

I am particularly indebted to Carla Fine, who labored tirelessly
through research, hours of interviews, and reams of transcripts and
whose dedication, writing, and editorial skills made this book what

ACKNOWLEDGMENTS

it is. I also greatly appreciate the encouragement, vision, and determination of my agents Barbara Lowenstein, and Madeleine Morel.

My sincere gratitude to my editor at Ballantine, Maureen O'Neal, for her support and guidance and for believing in this project not once, but twice. Special thanks to Steven Gutierrez for his efforts on behalf of this book, especially his attention to detail. Also, my thanks to Ruth Ross and Sigrid Estrada for the cover.

Finally, I wish to honor the legacy of the Hispanic pioneers who made it possible for the rest of us to be where we are today.

INTRODUCTION

Tu eres el arquitecto de tu propio destino.
You are the master of your own destiny.

I was speaking to the members of a Hispanic college leadership forum in Miami about developing strategies for succeeding in today's business world. As I looked out over the enthusiastic faces of these young men and women, the future leaders of the Latino community in the United States, I was reminded of how I, too, struggled eagerly for a piece of the American dream, eventually fulfilling the promise of professional recognition, personal satisfaction, financial prosperity, and the ability to contribute to the community that had enticed me as a college student.

After a short pause, I tore up my prepared notes, much to the surprise of my youthful audience, and shared with these bright and eager Latino students straight from the heart: "It is true that whatever success I may now enjoy is due to a lot of hard work and preparation. The effort, however, that I have put forth pales in comparison to the sacrifices of those who came before me, those whose legacy has made it possible for me, and you, to be where we are today. I have done my part, no doubt, but I am aware that I carry a debt of gratitude to all those who dared to dream and challenged me to do so, too; to my mother's prayers and to the generosity of people who shared their knowledge with me as I have made my way along my corporate journey."

The ensuing dialogue began the odyssey of this book and the privilege of walking with scores of Hispanic professionals at all levels of the corporate hierarchy. We shared experiences, concerns, dreams, and realities. We taught, learned, coached, and listened. This book, this guide, brings together these experiences to help you, so that we can help each other. There's some information you need to know if you choose to take a corporate journey. It's not about telling you who to be. You know who you are.

We are Latinos. Or is it Hispanics? Hispanos? Chicanos? Ibero Americans? Cubanos? Mexicanos? Centro Americanos? *Borricuas*? La Raza? *Hermanos*? We are each of these, and we are all of these. *Todos somos uno.* We are one. And we are where the action is. We are where the future is.

We Latinos are quickly becoming one of the most important groups in the United States. Our presence and influence are increasing in the political, cultural, social, and business arenas. Just look at the statistics:

- Americans of Hispanic origin (from Mexico, Puerto Rico, Cuba, Dominican Republic, Central and South America, and Spain) are the fastest-growing segment of the country's population. According to the 1996 U.S. census, Hispanic Americans will surpass blacks as the largest minority by the year 2005.
- One out of every four Americans—or 25 percent of the population—will be Hispanic by the year 2050, up from 10.7 percent in 1996. Latinos will also outnumber the nation's total of blacks, Asian Americans, and Native Americans combined.

- The Hispanic population is geographically concentrated in fourteen metropolitan areas of five states: California, Texas, New York, Florida, and Illinois.
- The predominant groups in the Latino community are Mexican Americans (13.3 million), Puerto Ricans (2.6 million), and Cuban Americans (1 million).
- In 1995, 46 percent of the twenty-three million foreign-born people in the United States were of Hispanic origin.

Our impact on the country's economy is especially dramatic: according to the U.S. Bureau of Labor Statistics, Hispanics are the most rapidly expanding ethnic market in the country, with a purchasing base of $190 billion a year.

As the strength of the Latino community becomes more and more apparent, businesses throughout the United States are beginning to realize that not only is it the right thing to hire and promote us, it is the smart thing. Yet as increasing numbers of Latinos enter the workforce with impressive educational and professional credentials, we are finding that only limited opportunities for advancement within our organizations are available to us. Much of this lack of opportunity is caused by the perception that we do not have what it takes to become corporate leaders. In fact, even though there are over two million Hispanic Americans who hold bachelor's and/or advanced college degrees, the national Glass Ceiling Commission found that most chief executive officers of major corporations believe that there is only a small pool of Latinos with the necessary credentials for top management positions.

CULTURE CLASH

Although mainstream America is starting to acknowledge the importance of the Latino community, we are not easy to categorize or understand. We Latinos come in all shapes and sizes, from lots of different backgrounds. We have many things in common but are extremely diverse. We tempt researchers and marketers to lump us all together, and then we drive them crazy with our different tastes and customs. The richness and diversity of Latino culture does not always translate well into the host culture of corporate America, which emphasizes sameness and predictability.

For Latinos, one of the greatest barriers to climbing the corporate ladder is the stereotyping and discomfort with our cultural differences that make white midlevel and senior-level managers reluctant to mentor and promote Hispanic men and women. A 1994 survey by the Hispanic Policy Department Project found that corporate supervisors admitted to being uncomfortable with what they perceived as Hispanic differences—or even what they *expected* might be unfamiliar about the Latinos with whom they worked, even when no differences were immediately evident.

How can Latinos in corporate America break through the multitude of cultural barriers and stereotypes in order to rise through the ranks from junior to senior management? What obstacles reduce our chances of being sponsored into the critical informal networks within our companies that provide entry into the inner circle of decision making and power? And what essential unspoken rules and subtleties do the Hispanic man and woman in the business world need to know to crash through the glass ceiling that keeps us from moving beyond a certain level of responsibility and into the forefront of corporate leadership?

To succeed in the corporate world, we Latinos must fight the perception that we are foreigners. We have to make hard choices about goals and values and learn to blend the cultures of our Latin heritage and our corporate community.

BLEND, DON'T BALANCE

To be Hispanic is to share a common bond—a bond that is based on our love of country, love of family, love of heritage, and love of tradition. The context of our cultural background is an integral part of who we are. Yet in order to participate and succeed in the corporate environment, we are often called upon to sacrifice parts of our Latino identity that we esteem and respect.

Because I have learned to look and act and speak and dress and have a lifestyle similar to others in corporate America, I am considered a businessman who happens to be a Latino, as opposed to a Latino businessman. I am now an "insider" in a world where individuals tend to hire, promote, and mentor those with whom they share similar backgrounds. I am accepted by my supervisors and peers, most of whom are white men, because I have learned to *blend*—not balance—the culture and value system that are part of my Hispanic identity with the realities of corporate life.

Just Because I'm Latin Doesn't Mean I Mambo offers practical advice and instructional guidance—including the unwritten rules and codes—essential for confronting the cultural stereotypes and hurdles that stand in the way of the Latino professional looking to be promoted. The book also deals directly with the fact that our culture and value system may have to be compromised in our climb up the corporate ladder. To succeed, we must take responsibility for who we are, not just shift the responsibility to the decision makers and expect them to change their views and stereotypes about us.

You, the reader, will have to ask yourself: How badly do I want this? What price am I willing to pay? How much am I willing to give up? This book, through inside information that is not taught in business school nor found in the current literature, will help you create a structure and a formula for navigating your way to the upper echelons of management. Once you are armed with this knowledge, it will be up to you to decide what you are willing to do to achieve success in your professional life and to be accepted—and eventually promoted—by the people for whom you work.

Legacy has always been a very interesting concept for me. I believe that often when we do the work that we do, we should think of it not only in terms of ourselves but also in terms of our children. That is a concept that we have used at the National Hispanic Employee Association: It is not only what we do for our children today but also what we do for the next seven generations of children.

I'm not so much concerned that corporate America or educational institutions or our government sectors create a better place for me now. But I definitely want to ensure that my daughter and my son and their children and their children's children have a better place to live. So the other issue for me is that I have a responsibility, a commitment, to try to create an environment whereby there is some work being done to plant the seeds to create a better legacy for future generations.

In that context, if I run across any opposition or if I run across anything "dangerous" for me politically or my career, I keep in mind what I want to leave for the future. This helps me put my problems in perspective. When I look back at my abuelos, who were farm workers and migrant laborers, I recall their vision was that someday one of their grandchildren would be a success.

The legacy that I want to leave for my children and future generations is very similar. I want them to have the opportunity to be presidents, CEOs, or anything else they choose to be without encountering a great deal of struggle.

—EDUARDO SALAZ
SENIOR HUMAN RESOURCES MANAGER
SILICON GRAPHICS & COMPUTER SYSTEMS

CHAPTER 1

KNOWING WHERE YOU COME FROM AND WHERE YOU ARE GOING

El que no sabe de donde viene, no sabe a donde va.
If you don't know where you come from,
you won't know where you are going.

You are about to embark on an exciting journey—a voyage that will take you far away from home, into an unfamiliar culture, and could make you a great success. But you will be challenged along the way. You will run into obstacles, will have to compete with others, and will have to prove your courage, intelligence, and dedication. To triumph, you must believe in yourself with unshakable pride and assurance.

Our Latino heritage can be a source of strength and self-esteem on your journey into America's executive offices and boardrooms. We are the descendants of achievers, men and women who were willing to take risks to realize their dreams. The mixture of our indigenous and European cultures has produced a proud and illustrious legacy: valor, loyalty, and commitment; intelligence, drive, and desire; a sense of nobility, adventure, and destiny. All of these are part of our birthright and will help you succeed.

So as you go forward into the corporate world, respect who you are and where you come from. Always value your Hispanic culture and traditions.

PRIDE IN OUR ROOTS

Antonio, a freshman at the University of Texas, comes home for spring break bursting with excitement. He has just joined a Mexican American political organization on campus and is pumped up with visions of Latinos exerting a greater influence in the upcoming national elections.

"Papá," he announces, "one of these days we're going to elect a Hispanic president of the United States. Just think of it, Dad, a Hispanic president."

The father, a Mexican immigrant with a sixth-grade education, looks at his son as if he were from the moon. "*Hijo*," he says, not understanding the kid's enthusiasm, "in my country, and everywhere in Latin America, *all* the presidents are Hispanic. Before *los güeros* [the Anglos] figured out which end of the boat was the front, our ancestors were performing surgery."

Antonio, who was born in the States, is a Hispanic American through and through. What's important to him is where Latinos are going in this country. His father, on the other hand, is still more rooted in the culture of his native country and carries with him the pride of centuries of achievement. We should not underestimate this pride, because it is a part of our heritage and gives us strength to create a vision for the future.

Our history is unique. It is a combination of the best of great cultures—that of the indigenous populations of the Americas, with their advanced systems of government and beliefs, and the Spanish settlers, with their tremendous desire to explore and extend their horizons.

When the Spaniards arrived, they came into contact with very stable and developed peoples, in all parts of the Americas. Each of the major cultures they encountered in present-day Mexico, Central America, and South America shared a wide range of accomplishments in such areas as agriculture, astronomy, and medicine, in addition to a rich spiritual life.

We are the sons and daughters of the union of these magnificent civilizations. We are the descendants of the movers and shakers of their time. And it is their legacy that we must live up to.

WE ARE THE ORIGINAL PIONEERS

> In entering the corporate world, you might be going somewhere that no one you know has ever been. Remember, though, that your ancestors also chose to enter uncharted territory. You are continuing in their spirit of adventure and courage.

The historical claim of the Hispanic people in the United States dates back to a time before the English even had their first permanent settlement in Jamestown. Our roots in this country were planted by groups of people from the interior of Mexico, who crossed some of the most treacherous land imaginable on foot and horseback to settle in Texas and the Southwest.

Their journeys took a lot of guts, a lot of brains, and a lot of determination. To mount the expeditions to get over here, to bring families, to bring supplies, these pioneers had to have organizational skills, the ability to lead, and a belief in themselves. To succeed, they had to be smart, motivated, enthusiastic. They had to be driven by the love of adventure and a burning desire to find out what was on the other side of the mountains.

This spirit of exploration is still a distinct characteristic of our culture. Many of us in the Hispanic community in the United States are descendants of the original settlers; many more of us can trace our roots to contemporary immigration. We share with our parents and grandparents the willingness to take risks for something we want for ourselves and our loved ones. Each of us is here because somewhere along the line someone in our family came looking for something different, something better, for more opportunity, more hope.

"My father came here from the Dominican Republic and worked in a factory," says Carlos, a young stockbroker from Dallas. "He always insisted that I should get an education and urged me to make something of myself. I didn't have the same advantages that most of my colleagues have had. Yet when I think of my father leaving his homeland, coming to a new country where he didn't know the language, working hard every day so that his children could better themselves, I know I, too, can make it in a world that is not familiar to me. I, too, am a trailblazer for my people. If you really want to work hard and achieve your goal, you have to be dedicated. You can achieve anything if you don't let others interfere with your dream."

Our background is inspirational. You should always remember our heritage to help you get where you want to go. If someone tells you that you cannot do something, that you are not educated enough, smart enough, ambitious enough, or experienced enough, do not let yourself be discouraged. Quite the contrary. Let it inspire you if someone says you can't—it should make you even stronger. *Querer es poder*—if you want it, you can do it. Whatever roadblocks you come up against do not begin to compare with those we as a people have had to overcome in the past.

Our ancestors did not know what was out there when they set off to make their home in the United States. Their journeys—filled with courage and willpower—remain our inspiration. They remind us that we have every right to prosperity, success, and respect. Their drive and desire and their willingness to take risks is our legacy. And it is these characteristics—which are valued and rewarded in business—that will help you succeed.

THE SPIRIT TO TAKE RISKS

> **The desire to explore and discover comes to us from our ancestors. What has changed are the frontiers that we now choose to face and conquer.**

For most Latinos, the corporate world is uncharted territory. But unlike our ancestors, the explorers and homesteaders, we have resources to help us navigate the unfamiliar terrain: education, access to information, opportunities to learn. We still may be pioneers, voyaging into the unknown, but we are now crossing the frontier in a jet instead of a covered wagon.

"My Hispanic roots ground me and remind me who I am," says Daniel, a senior communications executive. Raised in Texas, in a family that came to this country from Mexico, he believes the values he learned as part of his Latino heritage have helped him achieve success and recognition in his career.

"There is a very special picture that I keep on my bedroom dresser," he relates. "I am three years old and sitting on a swing set in front of my grandmother's home. It's a very humble house, set on wooden blocks, not even on a cement foundation. Every morning I wake up and look at the picture, so that I remember where I came from. I use that image to make sure that I don't let my work go to my head, that I don't let what I do and who I know grow out of proportion. It is important for me to always remember my roots because it gives me validation. I know my values are associated with my upbringing and have helped me become the successful person that I am today."

> By drawing on the spirit of our heritage, you can move forward with courage and strength.

THE DESIRE TO SUCCEED

> Our ancestors crossed oceans, climbed mountains, and settled new worlds. There is nothing you cannot do if you want it badly enough.

There are thousands of inspirational stories of Hispanics succeeding in every endeavor imaginable. What all of them have in common is the desire to succeed. Yes, there will be difficulties in your climb to the top of the corporate ladder. Yes, you will run into problems. Yes, there may be people who think that you don't deserve to be promoted, that you don't have the right credentials or the right experience. But our people's past is rich with courage and valor: if you truly decide to do something, you cannot be held back by any adversity.

You may be the first college graduate in your family. You may come from a background where no one has been in the business world before. You may not have had the same economic advantages as others or the social skills that would give you a leg up in corporate politics. But that shouldn't stop you, because you have the history that makes you who you are.

Andrea is a publishing executive in New York. Her parents came to the United States from Cuba, and she is the first college graduate in her family. "My mother taught me never to settle for anything," Andrea says. "She always told me to go for the best. She instilled in me the belief in pressing for what you deserve. To succeed in the corporate world, you must have the self-esteem that comes from having pride in your roots and your family."

The history of our people has been shaped by overcoming adversity—natural, geographic, and political. Whatever the obstacles you encounter, your heritage will always help you conquer them and triumph in the pursuit of your dreams.

LEGACY OF LEADERSHIP

> **To lead people, you have to believe in a vision and be able to communicate it in such a way that people will trust you and buy into your vision.**

Leadership is part of our legacy. Being aware of who you are will help you develop a vision of your own success, a vision of yourself as a leader in the corporate world. It's been said that there are very few extraordinary people, but a lot of ordinary people doing extraordinary things. If you believe in yourself and act out of that belief, others will believe in you as well and will follow your lead.

"I knew at an early age that I wanted to be important," says Rosario, a vice president at a Manhattan bank. "I was born in Mexico, raised on the border, and brought up in a traditional family," she explains. "When I went to Columbia University Business School in 1986, there was only one other Latino in my class. Although our culture teaches us to be modest about our accomplishments, I quickly learned that in order to succeed, I had to learn to speak up and self-promote. To become an insider, I realized I had to play by the rules of the business world.

"Even though the values I encountered in the corporate environment often conflicted with how I was raised, I always look to my Latino roots as a source of inspiration. In the most difficult of times, I think of my parents and imagine what it took for them to pick up and leave their home to come to the United States. It is their determination and courage that I call upon when I face the challenges of my work."

These are exciting times for Hispanics in the United States. Our many achievements in all fields—business, sports, government, medicine, entertainment, literature, academia, science—are proof that we are living up to our Latino heritage, to our legacy of leadership.

TAKING A STAND

> **If you don't stand for something, you will fall for anything. You have to take a stand.**

There are all kinds of business consultants out there right now, but I think the first one ever was probably Jethro, Moses's father-in-law. Why? Because one day he took Moses aside and said: "Moses, you know we're having some trouble here with the people. Forty years is a long time to be leading people through the desert on just charisma alone. At some point they are going to want to see a plan. And once that plan is formulated, it has to be communicated and sold."

So Moses headed for the mountains and came back with the Ten Commandments—a vision backed up by a plan!

It takes a lot of marketing to be able to get people to buy into your dream. A great deal of salesmanship is involved when you think big, I guarantee you.

You must plan your career with a can-do attitude, the fire in the belly, the drive and desire that define our culture and community. You should not stop your journey if you are told that you don't have the right experience for a job. You should not stop if you are told that you dress differently from everybody else. You should not stop if it is pointed out that you are not as fluent or articulate as your coworkers. You can address these obstacles. You can deal with them. You can work to overcome them.

Norman Vincent Peale said that if you can visualize it, you can make it happen. You have to start by believing that you really deserve to succeed, that you can make your dream come true. See yourself sitting behind an executive desk. See yourself giving a presentation to the stockholders, addressing the board of directors, leading your organization.

The only place to start is at the beginning. Our heritage boasts many people who did many more difficult things than trying to crack the ranks of management. You must draw on the power of their strength and conviction in order to make your vision of success and prosperity a reality.

Making changes, taking risks, seeking new paths, acting on your dreams: these are the characteristics of our ancestors. These attributes define who we are and where we came from. They motivate us and inspire us. They are the foundation of our heritage and the key to our success.

PEOPLE OF POWER, PEOPLE OF STRENGTH

We are the product of a unique blend of peoples. Our history must be our foundation. And now it is our job to add the bricks to create a structure for ourselves and our families.

As Latinos, we must come to terms with who we are, decide where we want to go, and work to accomplish our goals. We must use our bicultural and bilingual skills to our advantage, embracing the richness in our heritage to give us strength to choose our battles and strive for success.

You must remember, however, that success is not based on courage alone. You need an education, a degree, commitment, insight, knowledge, and exposure. You need inside information on corporate politics and etiquette. You must learn the unwritten rules that define the business world.

Predisposition is nothing without preparation.

First you must visualize your climb up the corporate ladder; then you must believe in it. In order to execute your goals, you must plan and prepare. You need a blueprint. Your success will be a result of the history and traditions that have come before you, the strengths and merit of your strategy, and the energy you invest in making your dreams a reality.

"All paths lead to the same goal, to convey to others what we are," writes the great South American poet Pablo Neruda. "We must pass through solitude and difficulty, isolation and silence, to reach the place where we can dance our dance and sing our song."

These words say a lot about who we are as Latinos and why we are here. Pride in our heritage and belief in our culture will prepare you to realize your dreams. You deserve nothing less. Knowing where you come from and where you are going is the first—and most important—step as you get ready to climb up the corporate ladder to success.

Look to your past
and you will see
the future:

Orgullo	Pride
Herencia	Legacy
Apoderamiento	Empowerment

Education is the great equalizer. Ask people to describe themselves and two things usually come up first: where they grew up and what school [college] they attended. Just as important are the credentials you keep in your tool chest. Education is the most critical tool, and not just for the sake of learning subjects. Arguably the most significant lifelong value acquired in school is the process of preparation, organization, socialization, and achievement in a competitive environment.

—LARRY ROMERO
DIRECTOR OF BUSINESS DEVELOPMENT
HISPANIC BUSINESS COLLEGE FUND

CHAPTER 2

PREPARING FOR THE CLIMB

Education, Conviction, Courage, y la Bendición

El que adelante no mira, atrás se queda.
If you don't look ahead, you'll stay behind.

"Ven, hijo, te doy la bendición." When I was a kid, these words used to make me cringe. No matter where I was going, my mother would intercept me and make the sign of the cross in the air above my head for the whole world to see.

"Mamá, por favor, no tan grande. Please, Mother, not so big," I would say to myself, worried about attracting people's attention. "I'm sure God, the Blessed Mother, and all the saints get the idea."

I did find consolation in seeing that all my Latino friends and schoolmates were also subjected to the public ritual of receiving their mothers' *bendiciones.* Sometimes in the schoolyard I fantasized that if our mothers synchronized their blessings, we all would levitate.

With time, I have learned to accept and cherish *la bendición* as an important part of a Latino religious tradition. I have also learned, however, that a successful journey is impossible without thorough preparation, even if we have our mothers' blessings.

La bendición is similar to the English saying "on a wing and a prayer," although I think they throw the "wing" thing in to fake us out! It is given when we have one foot out the door. So let's start outside the threshold of your mother's house. You have just received her *bendición* for your journey into the corporate world. It's time to start off—the rest is up to you.

KNOW WHERE YOU'RE GOING

Most people expend more *ganas* or energy on organizing a two-week vacation than they do on thinking through and planning their career paths. Yet if you don't have a clue where you're going, how will you know when you get there? Worse yet, how will you know if you wind up somewhere else?

> **To begin your journey into the upper levels of organizational management, you must prepare a road map that clearly shows the point from which you are starting out and where you want to end up.**

Let's use the example of planning a vacation. You have always wanted to see Miami. Fine, you know where you are going. Now, in order to figure out how you are going to get there, you have to know where you are going to start from. If you travel from Los Angeles, it is probably too far to drive, and you will have to fly. If you begin in New York, you can drive down in a couple of days. Whether you fly or drive, you have to make choices about your route, where you might want to stop along the way, how long you are willing to travel, how much money you can spend, and so on.

Planning your career, especially in the corporate environment, is very similar. You are pushing a product—and that product is you. Are you selling or marketing yourself? There is a difference.

In sales, we have a product and we take it to the marketplace in order to convince people to buy it. In marketing, we go into the marketplace first. We find out what people want and need. We research what presentation, type of packaging, and so on will work best. Then we come back and develop the product to satisfy the need.

> To succeed, you must *market* yourself. You have to know where you are starting from, where you want to end up, and how you are going to get there. You must devise a strategic plan for your climb up the corporate ladder and determine if you have the intelligence, drive, and courage for the journey.

DARE TO DREAM

As the saying goes, be careful what you wish for, because you might just get it. But what is it that you wish for? What is your dream?

Back in the old days, if your dad was a barber, you would most likely end up being a barber. If your family owned a *bodega*, chances were you too would run a grocery store. Now, the career options available to Latinos are wide open. We are succeeding in areas such as business, commerce, social services, government, and education. The sky's the limit. As Norman Vincent Peale says, "If you think you can, you can!"

The problem Latinos face when choosing a career in corporate America, however, is that most of us have no idea what this new world is all about. A good friend of mine, José—a very successful executive—told me that he always knew he wanted to work in a big company. He pictured himself sitting behind a huge desk, barking out orders, taking clients out to expense-account lunches at fancy restaurants. But in this mental picture, he was dressed in platform shoes and a white tuxedo, the most fashionable clothes his youthful mind could imagine.

Like José, many Hispanics don't know what they will encounter in their new environment. Corporate America is *la frontera*, the frontier. In the same way our ancestors entered uncharted territory to pursue their dreams, we find ourselves in unfamiliar surroundings, where we must learn to adapt in order to succeed.

Even today, most Latinos do not grow up with access to corporate culture or role models. Most of us do not attend prep schools and Ivy League universities, or have summer jobs in major organizations. When we fantasize about our success, we may not know enough about what really goes on in the executive suites to have a clear picture of what it takes to succeed.

The focus has always been on getting in. But you don't want to be like the dog who chases the car and, having caught it, doesn't have a clue what to do with it. In order to pursue your dreams, you must familiarize yourself with the environment you will be joining. You have to carefully construct a plan that understands and respects the culture in which you want to work, and be prepared to play by your organization's rules.

> **Dare to dream, but back it up with knowledge, self-awareness, and cultural flexibility.**

Pablo Picasso said, "My mother told me, 'If you become a soldier, you'll end up becoming a general; if you become a monk, you'll end up as the Pope.' Instead, I became a painter and wound up as Picasso."

SELF-ASSESSMENT INVENTORY

> **The first step to success is defining your dreams, interests, preparedness, and degree of motivation.**

A self-assessment inventory measures your *credentials*—such as educational background, technical skills, and outside interests—as well as intangibles like *courage* and *conviction*.

As you go forward with your assessment, you must constantly ask the hard questions:

- *¿Tengo coraje?* Do I have what it takes?
- *¿Y, a qué precio?* Am I willing to pay the price? Remember, cheap things are of little value; valuable things are never cheap.
- How many sacrifices will I be willing to make on the way up?

Knowledge is power. Those who have knowledge have power. In the corporate culture, information is the major commodity.

> **Controlling the dissemination of information ensures your rank within an organization.**

According to management consultant Peter Drucker, knowledge controls our access to opportunity and advancement. On a personal level, self-knowledge or awareness is critical to reaching your goals.

Start by taking a hard, honest look inside yourself. You must be painfully honest, especially about your strengths and weaknesses. Analyze your interests, your likes, your dislikes, your abilities, and your natural talents. If you have hobbies or leisure activities, think about why you do these things. What makes them enjoyable to you? Wouldn't it be wonderful if your career offered you the same satisfaction and enjoyment?

In this assessment, get help from others. Ask people close to you about what they see you doing in the future. Listen, but don't give in to pressures. The worst thing you can do is to choose a career to make someone else happy.

Use the following self-assessment inventory to start creating a road map for your career strategy. It will help clarify your goals and enable you to work toward achieving them with a defined, specific agenda.

Interest

Ask yourself what you really like to do. Visualize yourself doing it ten, fifteen, twenty years from now. How does it feel?

Studies indicate that people change careers several times during the course of their lives. Some of these changes are made by design; others are accidental.

> **When you are first starting out, you need to focus on those career decisions that are made by design.**

You want to make things happen, not merely watch what is going on around you.

Environment

After you've determined what you want to do, begin exploring the type of environment in which you would like to work. What surroundings make you feel the most comfortable? Do the products and policies of a certain company conflict with your values and standards? Make sure there's a good fit.

Education

How do you choose the right school to prepare for your career? The right degree? The school you attend will provide you not only with the necessary education but also with access to a network for future business relationships.

It will become apparent during your research that there are some top-notch business schools in the nation that are held in high regard. There are more people who want to get into them, how-ever, than there are seats available. So don't be shortsighted and prepare only one strategy based on getting accepted at one of these schools. There are many excellent schools, some public and some private, that offer a distinguished education in business. Have several plans ready—if plan one doesn't work out, you will be ready to go to plan two or plan three, or even plan four. You will be prepared.

A well-rounded education at the undergraduate level is an important first step in preparing for a business career. A strong liberal arts background will help you improve your written and verbal skills. In addition to business and accounting courses, study the classics, take speech classes, get involved in the debate club. Learn to speak clearly and write fluently. Merely majoring in business might help get your foot in the door, but without good communications skills and some knowledge of other subjects, you are likely to find yourself stuck in a job with no upward mobility.

Opportunity

You have to determine where to look for opportunities outside the academic arena.

> **Networking is an essential skill that you need to develop in order to be successful in the business world.**

You can learn to network in school and out of school, in organizations or in personal interaction, in activities on campus or off. You can learn by doing internships, by watching other people, by joining social, civic, and political organizations. You can get involved in athletics or volunteering for extra projects in the workplace. However you go about it, it is essential that you learn to meet people and tell them about your goals and ambitions.

Most Latinos grow up in environments removed from the world of business. Our fathers might be civil-service workers or mechanics. Our mothers might be teachers or full-time homemakers. We have to learn about corporate America from observing and listening to others.

"Both my parents were immigrants from Mexico—neither of

them finished high school—so they were really not able to guide me in my career," says Rosario, the Manhattan bank executive. "A lot of what I was doing I had to learn from what my friends were doing. I had to watch. I picked up things from reading, from television, from the guidance my friends were getting from their parents. But I didn't get it from my home. If anything, the message I was hearing from my family was that I should probably get married and have kids. And I just really didn't want to do that."

> In order to compensate for a lack of exposure, you have to put yourself in situations where you will have access to people who will be willing to act as mentors, role models, and guides along the way in your new environment. This process is essential in any career development plan.

Communication

In a recent survey of Latino executives, 95 percent of respondents ranked verbal communication as one of the most important skills for career advancement, and 76 percent cited written communication as one of the most important.

The essence of the corporate world is communication, both written and verbal. Even a poorly designed plan can be enhanced by the way it is presented.

There is a perception in some corporate environments that Hispanics don't speak or write English very well, that we are not very articulate. It is essential, therefore, that you do whatever necessary to strengthen and polish your communication skills.

> Our ability to motivate others is influenced by how we present our ideas. Communicating effectively in order to bring out the best in the people around us shows that we have the leadership qualities needed to succeed in the business world.

Ambition

You must ask yourself: Do I have what it takes? Do I have the ability to sustain a rhythm? Am I willing to pay the price? What motivates me? How much am I willing to pay for something that I really, really want?

You know, we're a people who have faced tremendous obstacles throughout our history. We are a people who have had to work harder to accomplish our goals—not for lack of intelligence, but for lack of opportunities.

If you are committed to advancing on your career path, you have to call on that same spirit of resilience and determination. A halfhearted effort means certain failure in your journey to success.

Choices

Look inside yourself to determine what it is that makes you want to succeed. How many sacrifices are you willing to make on the way up the corporate ladder? At what cost are you prepared to achieve the goals you have in mind? We all need to know what the game involves before we decide if we are willing to play. Make an honest assessment to judge whether you have what it takes.

> **You should not decide to compete unless you are prepared to win.**

Teamwork

In order to get ahead in the business world, you must learn to work as part of a team. You need to be willing to contribute to a common goal.

> **You have to be able to function in a "we" environment.**

In order to be a committed and successful player in the corporate world, you need to learn to exercise individual leadership within a team environment, much like the quarterback of a football team. Like a quarterback, you must be fully aware of everything taking place around you and have the capacity to spark the performance of others to achieve the team objective.

The Hispanic culture teaches us to be thoughtful of the opinions that others give us. It teaches us to be respectful of our parents and our elders.

> **You should honor the input you get from others, but you must also learn to look within yourself to determine your own interests and pursuits and to formulate a vision for yourself and your team. The decision to succeed is within you.**

PROFILE OF HISPANIC EXECUTIVES

The 1997 *Corporate Elite Directory*, compiled by *Hispanic Business* magazine, identified only 249 Hispanic executives at the level of vice president and above at Fortune 1,000 companies; all of them were concentrated at 145 corporations.

> **This means that Hispanics, while comprising 10 percent of the U.S. population, represent only 1.6 percent of the fifteen thousand managers at Fortune 1,000 companies. Hispanic women comprise only 0.25 percent of all these executives.**

There are eleven Hispanics at the CEO level, and five have reached the highest position at their companies: Tony L. White, Perkin-Elmer Corp.; Carlos H. Cantu, ServiceMaster Co.; David I. Funter, Office Depot, Inc.; the late Roberto C. Goizueta, Coca-Cola Co.; and Arthur C. Martinez, Sears, Roebuck and Co.

The typical Hispanic executive is a college-educated male

in his forties who has worked fourteen years at the same company. The commercial banking and telecommunications sectors employ the most Hispanic executives, followed by scientific, photographic, and control equipment; electronics; electrical equipment; publishing, printing; entertainment; food; and electric and gas utilities.

Sectors with no representation of Hispanic executives include advertising, marketing, brokerage, engineering, construction, forest and paper products, furniture, marine services, mining, crude-oil production, pipelines, railroads, textiles, transportation and equipment, and trucking.

In a recent survey about career beginnings, 29 percent of the executives who responded stated that their first professional job was engineering/technical; 16 percent, management trainee; 11 percent, other entry-level; 10 percent, accounting/financial; 5 percent, junior sales; 26 percent, other.

Forty-eight percent of the respondents said they obtained their first job in corporate America through regular college recruitment; 29 percent through networking or other personal contacts; 14 percent through an advertisement or want ad; 5 percent by cold calling; 2 percent through an internship; and 2 percent by other methods.

In addition, a 1996 report by the American Council on Education found that business is the fastest-growing field of study for Hispanic students. MBA programs with strong Hispanic representation have an increasing number of students who are working professionals looking to enhance their skills in specific areas such as finance, general management, or marketing, in order to advance in their organizations or make a career change.

Even though Latinos are underrepresented in the business world, the number of professional organizations for Hispanics continues to increase. There are presently more than twenty occupation-based groups for professionals, including the National Hispanic Employee Association, the National Hispanic Corporate Council, and the National Society of Hispanic MBAs.

In addition, there are many Hispanic employee associations. These groups allow Latino professionals to meet their coworkers, promote the work of the corporation within the Hispanic community, and provide educational and mentoring opportunities for Hispanics. Examples of Hispanic employee associations include that at AT&T, with a membership of 1,100; Ameritech, with a membership of 1,800; and US West Inc., with a membership of 900.

As more Latinos enter the corporate arena, our presence and influence will continue to grow. Our success will pave the way for others to follow in our footsteps.

FORMULA FOR SUCCESS

In my travels, I have had the opportunity to talk to many prominent Latino executives. The consensus is that all corporate success stories are about men and women who excel in the following areas:

- Knowledge
- Technical skills
- Access
- Communication
- Networking ability
- Desire
- Conviction
- Drive

In the pursuit of excellence, you will also need:

- Courage
- Mobility
- Dedication
- Ability to take risks
- Standards
- Values

- Flexibility
- Leadership skills
- Responsibility
- Ability to build relationships
- Ability to work in a team
- Decisiveness
- Ability to self-manage
- Social, civic, and recreational involvement outside the office
- Self-confidence and self-esteem
- Ability to find mentors and role models
- Intuition
- Ability to read your environment
- Creativity and innovation
- Drive to perform
- Flexibility and openness
- Ability to create an image
- Mental strength

These traits can be broken down into four components: what you are made of, whom you know, what you've learned, and where you've learned it.

What You Are Made Of

There will be a price to pay for success. Are you willing to pay it? Are you willing to invest the time and energy to attain your goals? Are you willing to sacrifice personal time for the sake of your career? Acquiring and developing the skills necessary to succeed in corporate America is not easy.

Whom You Know

The next thing you need to do is benchmark—identify successful individuals whom you would like to emulate and learn how they made it. Make lists of people who might be helpful in developing a career strategy. Identify mentors and role models, including people in and outside of your chosen field. Find individuals who can offer you practical advice and those who can offer you hands-on opportunities to gain experience and get a feel for your career.

What You've Learned

The key to success is knowledge and information. Always ask yourself what you will need to know to get ahead. The corporate world is fiercely competitive and knowledge-based. Academic achievement is essential. Realize that in certain fields an advanced degree will be necessary, while in others what you learn on the job will have as much weight.

Where You've Learned It

Knowledge is not obtained only in an academic setting. Observe successful people at your company and other organizations. Read business magazines and journals. Attend seminars and conferences. Your education does not end once you leave the campus. Remember, we learn throughout our lives.

DIVERSITY VS. AFFIRMATIVE ACTION

At progressive companies throughout the country, diversity policies are replacing affirmative action programs. Although these two approaches are not interchangeable, their goals of increasing the number of people of color and women within organizations are similar.

> **While affirmative action is a legislative approach usually limited to specific categories and numbers of employees based on race and gender, diversity stresses individual differences as a strength within the corporate culture.**

Diversity focuses on corporate attitude and includes recruitment, promotion, and hiring, and enhances the success of the organization by recognizing and valuing different perspectives and contributions resulting from different cultural backgrounds. Broadening a company's market base and supplier network are also important goals of diversity programs.

In a survey conducted by *Hispanic Business* magazine, 85 percent of respondents said that their corporations have a diversity initiative in place and felt that their company's efforts at diversity outreach are sincere. Forty-five percent said that the diversity efforts in their companies have either helped their careers "significantly" or "helped somewhat."

There has been somewhat of a backlash against affirmative action and diversity initiatives. This reaction is based on the perception that these programs are designed to make the white majority population—the host culture of corporate America, so to speak—feel guilty. But the reality is that all they do is level the playing field. Once we get our foot in the door, it is our responsibility to perform.

> **We need to break those barriers that exist within, so we can confront the barriers that exist outside. *Apodérate*—It's all about empowerment.**

Before you join a company, find out what its official policy and informal reputation are regarding promoting and advancing women and people of color. The glass ceiling is alive and well, and some organizations are known to be more receptive than others to diversity within their ranks.

NAVIGATING TWO WORLDS

When Latinos begin work at a corporation, they quickly become immersed in two separate worlds—one business, one personal.

Learning how to navigate in these separate worlds is an essential lesson on your way up through management.

Our backgrounds and experiences are rooted in a culture very different from the one that exists in business. The corporate world has its own rules, values, and standards—ones that are foreign to most of us in the Hispanic community.

To succeed, you must understand that you are now a member of two separate societies. And you must learn: learn the values of your organization, learn what drives and motivates the organization, learn to acculturate yourself to the organization. You must understand the concept of the organization as *familia*, a family unit with its own history, tradition, rules, responsibilities, and so on.

The difficulty comes in reconciling your two different cultures. As you immerse yourself in the corporate world, you might be forced to give up some of your old ways. You may come to realize that you don't have the same degree of support from family and friends that you had before. You may have no one to talk to about what you are experiencing, because the people closest to you may not understand what you are going through. Your parents, your close friends, the community where you grew up are probably very far removed from your new culture. And it can become very lonely at times.

As a result, you may feel as if you are developing a split personality, constantly shifting between the corporate culture of your new job and the Latino culture of your home and community.

> **You must be careful not to be held back by feelings of guilt at leaving your roots or by people who might be threatened by your decision to succeed in your chosen career path.**

At times, you might find yourself struggling against distancing yourself from the people who are nearest and dearest to you. You may suddenly find that you have to make hard decisions. For example, Marco is a banking executive from Dallas who became a vice president of his company within several years of being hired. Even after he moved to an exclusive part of the city, he would return to his old neighborhood on weekends to hang out with his friends. They would kid him about "selling out," teasing him that he had become too important to live near his family. They would comment on his clothes, his new haircut, the way he spoke.

Marco found himself slowly starting to pull away from his old *barrio*. He began spending his free time with people from his new neighborhood or with his coworkers. Although he felt guilty about neglecting his past ties, Marco soon came to realize that he could be more helpful to his people through his achievements and visibility as a successful Latino executive.

Why would Marco's success help and enhance the Latino community? Because he was now in a position to contribute in a very constructive way, both financially and in his role as a mentor to a younger generation of Hispanics who were looking to him for connections and advice on entering corporate America.

ASSIMILATION, ACCULTURATION, BICULTURATION

When we enter a foreign culture, we look for a way to fit in. There are several ways of doing this: we might assimilate, acculturate, or biculturate, depending on the environment and our predisposition.

When you assimilate, you give up the traits of your culture and take on the traits of the dominant culture. Some Latinos are comfortable with this choice. To integrate fully into the corporate world, they let go of all ties with their own culture.

Acculturation is another way—and the most common—of balancing the environment of your job and your Hispanic background. Acculturation is defined as the modification of a culture as it comes into contact with another culture. In this process, you take on certain traits of the host culture but don't let go of the essential characteristics of your heritage.

Some people biculturate, creating a hybrid culture that has the most positive traits of each. Marco, for example, knew that he could only accomplish his goals by blending his two worlds, incorporating into his corporate life the Latino values of drive, ambition, and loyalty that were ingrained in his upbringing.

The growing importance of the knowledge of foreign languages in today's global business environment illustrates the need for cultural adaptation. We Latinos should have a natural advantage, because Spanish is emerging as the most commonly spoken language on earth. But the perception in the corporate world that all Hispanics are fluent in Spanish actually puts some of us in a negative light.

If we grew up bilingual and are very strong in English and Spanish, we are ahead of the game. But there were many Latinos who did not learn Spanish because their parents wanted their children to grow up assimilated. Therefore, it is especially important for Hispanic executives to have a mastery of Spanish. All of our communication skills should be highly polished—whether it be our native language, or our second language, or even a third or fourth language. I advise anyone in the corporate world to speak at least one other language, and Spanish is an excellent language to know.

Language is the most important measure of how well you fit in. So being highly articulate in English cannot be overemphasized for anyone who is hoping to succeed in business. Do whatever you can to improve your speaking and writing skills.

In developing a career, those people who stick with what they know and do what they've always done will never progress beyond a certain point. You need to be open to new ideas and be flexible enough to pick and choose the best traits of each culture to help you succeed.

Know who *you* are. Learn who *they* are. Then blend the positive aspects of both worlds.

BUILDING RELATIONSHIPS

Success in the corporate world is based to a large degree on relationships. For a company to be effective and profitable, strong relationships need to exist among the people who work there; between the organization, its customers, and its suppliers; and between the company and the communities in which it operates. The Latino culture is also relational, one that is based on how well people get along with each other. The ability to forge good relationships is part of our heritage; it is not something we need to learn.

> **Drawing on the examples of our Latino upbringing, you must build relationships, and build them early on in your career. These lasting relationships will help you move ahead in your organization.**

Executives seek out, select, and promote those individuals with whom they feel most comfortable. They will promote not a perfect stranger but a person they know, can relate to, feel good about, and count on—people they trust.

To build business relationships, you need to connect with individuals who can help you chart and develop your career path. And you must be proactive in finding and approaching these mentors and role models. Rarely will anyone come to you. You have to go out and seek them.

> **Every job I've had, every promotion I've gotten, every contract I've secured, every presentation I've been asked to give, was the result of someone recommending me, someone knowing me, someone trusting me.**

You can't be uncomfortable approaching people and sharing your goals and desires with them. Talking to someone about a goal of yours is a powerful motivator, because making it public drives you to accomplish it. By sharing your dreams with others, you assume a greater responsibility for making those dreams come true. People watch you. They ask: "How are you doing? Are you getting there? Are you reaching the goals you set for yourself?" Keeping your dreams and goals private is a cop-out, because you don't have to answer to anyone. You can protect yourself from any embarrassment by keeping your ambitions secret. But ultimately you will have to answer to yourself for either success or failure. There are no self-made successes, only self-made failures.

SELF-PROMOTING IS NOT BOASTING

Latino culture tells us not to call a lot of attention to ourselves. We grew up with the idea that if we always do our best—if we work hard, if we study hard—then good things will come to us. But in order to succeed in the corporate world, you must also learn how to promote yourself. You must understand that if you never ask to be noticed, you will never be noticed. So you must overcome our Latino emphasis on modesty and the fear of calling attention to ourselves. You must learn to take the risk of making yourself known.

In my first job, I believed that if I merely worked hard, my work would be noticed. But I quickly found that other people would take credit for my work unless I was able to promote myself. I had to learn to make people realize that this was *my* work—it was a project that *I* had completed. In any organization, there are those people who call the shots and those who do the work. The ones who rise to the top and call the shots are the ones who are best at promoting themselves and their accomplishments.

READING THE ENVIRONMENT

The ability to read the environment of your organization is essential in preparing for your climb up the ladder of success. You must learn to recognize the power structure and be aware of the office dynamics.

> **Every organization has both a formal and an informal structure. The formal structure is the organizational chart, with its listing of the hierarchy of executives. The informal structure is the network of key players who make the power decisions in the organization.**

In order to find a mentor in your company, you must align yourself with those individuals who are on their way up. When I was starting out, I wanted to learn from and be mentored by the best. I looked at the path I wanted to pursue, then identified the different supervisors who could help advance my career. I realized that the head of my division—who was a very capable individual—would not be able to provide me with the growth opportunity that I needed to succeed. So I identified the executive whom I most wanted to emulate and learn from and who was in the best position to help promote *my* career.

Before making a move, I did my homework. I conducted research about his career and learned about his approach to business and marketing. So even though I was a total stranger when I approached him at a business meeting, he was impressed by how much I knew about his department and career. I told him of my long-term plans and of my desire to work under his tutelage. I explained how I believed my skills would contribute to his division. I came fully prepared.

I was careful not to burn any bridges behind me. I was very complimentary about the individual for whom I was working at the time. I explained that I had learned a tremendous amount from that person but felt that his career path was not the one I wanted to emulate. I told my future mentor that I believed he was the best person to help me.

People like to hear good things about themselves, especially those that are specific and true, and my future mentor was impressed by my thoroughness. He sensed my desire to advance my career by modeling it after his. And, luckily for me, we just clicked.

Even though I was brought up to be modest, not to toot my own horn, I was willing to risk looking pushy, because I saw that this was the way people got ahead in my organization. It was difficult calling attention to myself. But in the corporate world, you have to be willing to say: "Hey, how about me? Try me. Let me do it." You have to stand up and say: "I want to get up to bat. Put me on your team."

If this man had turned me down, it would have been difficult for me to do this again with another mentor candidate. But it would have been necessary. As it turned out, he contacted me shortly after our talk and helped me transfer into his division.

In every organization, some areas offer more opportunities for advancement than others. Let's say, for example, that the majority of the senior executives in your organization started out in marketing, finance, or sales. Assuming you have the skills and background to excel in one of these areas, you should select a mentor who is plugged into the power and influence structure of that division. Then you must convince him or her to guide you along and promote you within the organization.

It is important to pick an individual who is willing to bring people along. In some organizations, executives tend to be very protective of their territory. In others, individuals at the top are actually rewarded for identifying and developing up-and-coming talent. If your company has the kind of environment that encourages mentoring, you have a better chance of getting the help you will need to get ahead.

By reading the environment of your organization, you will empower yourself to act in a manner that will be considered not only appropriate but admirable. And you will find the opportunities for success.

COURAGE TO ACT

Courage is the ability to look inside yourself and see if you have what it takes to make tough decisions: the ability to take risks by putting your neck and your feelings on the line. Ultimately, courage is the ability to act in spite of fear.

Knowledge and information are the best allies in facing down your fears. If you are afraid of something, the best thing to do is learn more about it, so you can deal with it. If you're scared of giving presentations in front of a crowd, for example, take a public-speaking course to learn the techniques of coping with stage fright. If numbers intimidate you, take an accounting course to build confidence.

"My first job out of college was at a major brokerage firm, and I experienced total culture shock," says David, a young stockbroker from New York. "I had never been exposed to the type of people who worked in that environment, and it just took me by surprise. Although I felt scared and insecure, I observed how they dressed, how they spoke, how they interacted with each other, and then I imitated them. I always tell people that the first two years I worked there, I learned the most important lesson of my career: I learned how to carry myself in the corporate setting. I thought of walking out the door many times but made myself stay because I didn't want to be considered a quitter."

If you are like the majority of Latinos, you did not grow up with the advantages of others in corporate America. To compensate, we need to seek out people who can help us by telling us what to do and how to do it.

"I remember the first time I learned to knot a tie," says Daniel, the California communications executive. "I was going to my freshman prom, and I had never worn a tie before in my life. My parents, although born in the United States, still spoke the Spanish of their native Mexico. They were very humble people, very proud and energetic, and always set good examples for me in terms of role models.

"I borrowed a suit and tie for the prom from a friend. The night of the dance, I went to my dad and asked him to help me knot the tie. My father was a machinist who had worked himself up from digging ditches for the state of Texas. He didn't even own a tie and told me to ask my mom if she could give me a hand. She couldn't figure it out, either. But then she remembered that my uncle was a musician in a band and wore a tie. So I called my uncle, who said yes, he could help me.

"I went to see my uncle at his club, and he took out three ties and told me to pick the one I wanted. They all already had knots in them—my uncle didn't know how to tie one, either!

"In the end, I was lucky. My date's older brother helped me. That night I felt I had arrived at a certain turning point in my life. I looked in the mirror and thought the tie made me look like a business executive. I liked the way it looked.

"It might seem insignificant, but that night taught me that there were people outside my immediate environment who could give me advice and show me the way into a different world from the one I knew."

Your success in reaching upper management will depend on your having the strength to say you don't know, the courage to ask for help, the dignity to accept advice, and the power to use the Hispanic culture as a source of inspiration to accomplish your goals.

To get there from here:

Dream

Evaluate

Educate

Implement

Play the game! The more you talk like "they do," the more you dress like "they do," and the more you share like "they do," the more successful you'll be. Usually you only have one shot at making a lasting impression. Make it count! Don't give them reasons to exclude you from the game before it starts.

—VICTOR ARIAS JR.

EXECUTIVE VICE PRESIDENT

AND MANAGING DIRECTOR

DHR INTERNATIONAL, INC.

CHAPTER 3

JUST BECAUSE I'M LATIN DOESN'T MEAN I MAMBO
What You Need to Know About Stereotypes

De músico, poeta, y loco, todos tenemos un poco.
Every person has a bit of musician, poet, and madman in them.

Some years ago I was transferred by my company. In preparation for the move, I scouted out several residential areas. With two young children the top priority, an area that was within the finest school district was chosen. This was a covenant community, with houses in the $200,000–$500,000 range and plenty of gardens and lawns, a clubhouse, a pool, tennis courts, a lake, a park, and playgrounds. It was far enough from the city to offer a good country life but close enough to allow us to take advantage of the best the city had to offer. The house we bought was in a safe cul-de-sac and promised fantastic property value appreciation.

The community was a favorite with corporate relocation firms, and many of the houses were occupied by executives who had transferred into the area. My boss, who lived in a community of country estates about five miles down the road, also endorsed the choice.

The only drawback I could see was that the neighborhood seemed a little sterile. There were only two other Hispanic families among the five hundred families living in the community.

One evening, shortly after we moved in, the phone rang. When I answered, a chipper female voice said: "Hello, my name is Chris. I live in the house across the cul-de-sac from you. We recently moved here and are just beginning to explore the area. My husband and I just love Mexican food, and the realtor said you might tell us which is the best Mexican restaurant in town."

I had yet to say a word. Did she really love Mexican food and mistakenly believe that I was the food critic for the local newspaper? Did she think that I had done better research about the area and knew all about the local restaurant scene? Or was she trying to confirm that a Hispanic family—with two young children who did not speak English—had moved into this executive enclave?

"I'd love to help you, Chris," I replied, "but to tell you the truth, I don't eat Mexican food."

My words were greeted with silence, then a nervous giggle. "Oh, I get it," she said. "You're kidding, right? I mean, you probably don't eat it in restaurants, you must cook it at home."

"Nope, too spicy," I said. "I prefer low-cal, fat-free things myself, salads and such. However, should I hear any recommendations at work, I'll be sure to pass them along. And by the way, forgive my lack of manners. I never introduced myself. My name is Juan. *Adiós!*"

> **Stereotypes are out there. You must acknowledge and deal with them.**

PRECONCEIVED IMAGES

In order to succeed in the corporate arena, you must recognize that there are preconceived images about the Latino culture that will impact and influence your career. To avoid playing into these notions of who you are and how you'll act, you need to understand what a stereotype is and the most common ones that Hispanic men and women confront on their way up the corporate ladder.

Stereotypes are generalized beliefs that certain behaviors and characteristics are typical for members of a particular group. So if you are Hispanic, or African American, or Jewish, or Asian American—you can fill in the blanks here—you are expected to act a certain way, speak a certain way, be a certain way.

Stereotypes are used by people as labels to categorize other people, and they influence:

- How you perceive others
- How others perceive you
- How you treat others
- How others treat you

> **It is very important to remember that stereotypes are based on perception, not reality.**

You do not actually have to have any of the expected characteristics to be stereotyped. The reason for this is that these expectations can be traced back to core beliefs or values that people develop very early on in their lives. Therefore, the perception becomes the reality.

A study conducted at the University of Colorado found that by the time we are ten years old, 90 percent of our values are in place. By the time we are twenty-one, the other 10 percent are locked in.

Therefore, our ideas about the world around us are formed when we are at our most impressionable. As we grow, we're bombarded by information, and it is these images and notions that we use as building blocks for our conceptions of people and things.

If we look at how Latinos are generally portrayed, we can see that there is lots of material for negative stereotypes. The image of the Hispanic in the popular imagination is patterned on the Frito Bandito, "Miami Vice" bad guys, movie-screen drug lords, and Ricky Ricardo.

Take comic books, for example. I loved them as a little kid, but when I look back I realize that despite seeming innocent enough, they really carried some very negative messages. My favorite at the time was Donald Duck. Donald's little nephews— Hucy, Dewey, and Louie—always got tangled up in exciting adventures. More often than not, they were going into Third World countries, usually Latin, to overthrow a nasty dictator.

So you have these little kids—little white American ducks— going in and resolving all the problems of a Latin country. The message an impressionable child gets from this is that being white puts you in a leadership role. You're automatically a problem solver, and you have to take care of people who are too inept to help themselves.

Stereotypes are also passed from one generation to the next. What we learn from our parents is very important. If the parents in a white family tell their children to lock the doors and roll up the windows when they drive through a predominantly Hispanic part of town, the kids will probably be more likely to grow up thinking of Latinos in negative terms.

In the business world, where relationships and trust are of great importance, stereotypes can be especially damaging to advancing your career. In what is called the "Pygmalion effect," people who are expected to do well perform measurably better than those who are expected to fail. So if the top managers of your organization have negative images of Latinos, they will probably expect certain types of behavior from them, and the stereotypes could become self-fulfilling prophecies.

> You have to know what the stereotypes are and act in a way that proves them wrong. You owe it to yourself and to the generations of Latinos who will follow you in corporate America.

GLASS CEILING EFFECT

The Glass Ceiling Commission, a federal panel that studied the barriers faced by women and nonwhite ethnic and racial groups in corporate America, found that the major hurdles Hispanic-Americans encounter in the private sector include:

- The perception among CEOs that there is only a small pool of Hispanic men and women with the credentials required to move up the career ladder
- Business recruitment practices that overlook or do not identify Latinos who have the necessary credentials
- Entry-level discrimination that steers Hispanics into staff positions, as opposed to line positions, and holds them there
- A tendency to consider potential Hispanic recruits in terms of Spanish-speaking markets (this discriminates against the five million Hispanic Americans eighteen years of age and older who do not speak Spanish at all or do not speak it well)
- Insensitivity on the part of executives to cultural differences
- Stereotyping and discomfort with cultural differences that make white middle-level and senior-level managers reluctant to mentor and promote Hispanic men and women
- Absence of a significant pool of Latino mentors for Latinos trying to advance
- Isolation from informal communication networks
- Lack of assignments that provide visibility and interaction with senior managers

> **The commission also found that while CEOs express the conviction that including Hispanics at *all levels* is good for the bottom line, Latinos perceive a limit on how far they are allowed to go.**

Stereotypes of Hispanics are widespread in corporate America, and the Glass Ceiling Commission reported that Latinos are generally lumped together and widely perceived as poor, uneducated, and recently arrived in the United States. The commission also reported that Hispanic males are stereotyped as chauvinistic, domineering, arrogant, prone to violence, unwilling to learn English, and not patriotic about the United States. Latinas are frequently seen as strong, stoic, self-sacrificing, tied to family and community, dominated by their husbands and fathers, passive, overly emotional, and undereducated.

> **Although the stereotypes of Hispanic men and women are different, they put all Latinos in a negative light when considered as potential candidates for corporate leadership.**

Fausto, a human resources executive, recalls:

"The first time I realized I was different because I was Latino was in college. I went to a high school that was predominantly Latino. It was a very comfortable setting. When I went to college, there were twenty-six thousand students, and only a very small percentage were Latino.

"In corporate America, I have not encountered outright discrimination, but I have witnessed subtle stereotyping.

"People have specific stereotypes about Latinos that are not shared. They look at us as if we can only do so much, that we may not aspire to certain areas, that we don't have the capability to do certain things. I believe that Latinos have to work three times as hard just to be on an equal footing with a lot of other folks. I think it is apparent from people's beliefs that they are not intentionally evil but that they just have some very stereotypical beliefs that they have been brought up with.

"A long time ago I realized that after it is all said and done, all you have is your family and your culture. When your corporation downsizes you, or lays you off, or when you move to another corporation, ultimately all you have to rely on is who you are. And if you can be about giving back, if you can be about taking a stand and being a revolutionary about change and creating change, then you can ultimately hang your hat on that and say no matter what I do or where I am, I have made a difference. And that is what is ultimately important."

OVERCOMING DISCRIMINATION

Not too long ago, on a business trip to Nebraska, I went to see a college friend who is now a marketing executive with a large agribusiness firm. On the day we agreed to meet, I went to his office and announced myself to the receptionist. I was asked to wait. A few moments later, his secretary came out to tell me that he was in a meeting but had asked her to give me his house keys. He said I should go to his house to "do what I needed to do" and that he would be along shortly. I had given my friend little notice that I was in town, so I was not surprised that I had to wait for him at his home while he juggled his schedule to see me.

My friend, for his part, was very surprised to find me sitting in his living room two hours later. "What are you doing here?" he asked, "and where have you been? I've been waiting for you at the office—we were supposed to go out for lunch." I told him that his secretary had given me the keys, directions, and his instructions to come to his home and "get started."

My friend burst out laughing. "She must have thought you were the painter," he said. "I told her that I was having my house painted and that a contractor was coming to the office to pick up my keys so he could get started on the job. His name is Juan, too."

"Yeah, I guess we all look the same," I answered. "But does your painter wear a suit and tie?"

Although we were old friends and were able to joke about the mix-up, discrimination—both overt and subtle—is no laughing matter.

Most Hispanic executives experience or have experienced discrimination. Many Latino men have told me they dread black-tie business functions, for instance, because they are often mistaken for waiters at formal dinners and receptions.

The reality is that we, as Latinos, do not enter the workplace with a clean slate. We must work hard to overcome the preconceived notions that our employers and coworkers—the majority of whom are white males—have about us.

I have a Puerto Rican friend who, on starting a new job, noticed that all his projects were being closely monitored and micromanaged. When he finally got up the courage to ask one of his bosses what was going on, he was told that they just wanted to make sure that he would be able to complete his work in a timely and appropriately professional fashion.

"You know," his boss said somewhat apologetically, "you're the first Puerto Rican we've ever had at the company, and we really don't know what to expect."

But my friend knew immediately what they were probably anticipating. His supervisors had the stereotypical image of Puerto Ricans as lazy and not reliable with time management. As a result, his supervisors were uneasy about assigning him a task and letting him run with it. The underlying expectation was that because he was Puerto Rican, he would not do well.

My friend knew that to prove the stereotype wrong, he had to work harder, hand his projects in earlier, and be more efficient than his coworkers. He had to show the power structure of his company that he was not the way they expected him to be.

Many Latinos grow up in sheltered environments. You might live in a city or neighborhood that is predominantly Hispanic or attend a mostly Latino school. Maybe you were raised in a country where Latinos are the dominant group. You might not be aware of the preconceived notions some Americans have about Latinos. But these negative stereotypes—some of them racist and discriminatory—are out there, and you have to be prepared to deal with them in your professional life.

"Even though discrimination is not as overt as it used to be, it still exists," says Ramón, a vice president of a national computer organization. "A lot of people have learned to give Academy Award performances of getting with the program, but deep down inside they don't really believe in diversity. They might know the right things to say in front of the right people, but it's not genuine. Even so, I firmly believe that it is up to us to break through the discrimination and stereotypes. It is our job to show them we are different from their preconceived images of Hispanics. Whether we like it or not, we are teaching them about our people. The degree to which we change their views will affect the other Latinos who come after us."

> **Stereotypes are often based on some fragment of truth—they reflect differences in values and priorities. Yet each of us is unique and should be evaluated on our merits. We are all responsible for proving ourselves and disproving the negative stereotypes associated with the Hispanic community.**

COMMON STEREOTYPES

Rosa María has an MBA from Stanford. She is a vice president of the finance department at an automotive-industry manufacturer located outside a large metropolitan area with a significant Latino population.

Rosa María is well liked and respected at her company. Even so, she constantly has to put up with negative comments about the Hispanic community. Many of these come as backhanded compliments. If there is a news item about crime in the inner city, for example, she is told that she is not like "those people." If there are problems with the predominately Hispanic and African American rank-and-file employees, she hears: "I wish they were more like you—you're different."

Deep down, Rosa María does not feel any different from "those people," save for the choices she made and the sacrifices her parents made. And she knows that there are thousands of others like her in the Latino community who would succeed if given half a chance. So every time she hears, "I wish we had ten of you," she replies, "You can. Go recruit them!"

> **Hispanics in the corporate world face a wide array of stereotypes about our culture. Don't get angry—get educated. Know what people may be thinking about you and show them by your actions and attitude who you really are and how you can contribute to the company.**

Some of the common stereotypes about Latinos include:

1. *We are uneducated.* The idea still persists that educated Latinos are the exceptions to the rule. So those of us who do have bachelor's or master's degrees are often viewed as having made it to where we are because of affirmative action rather than merit.

"I have my master's degree in business from Harvard, and there are still people in the company who think I got my job—and my education—only because of a quota," says Felipe, an executive at a leading insurance company. "I don't think it would make a difference if I hung my diploma on my office wall. There's still this perception that most Hispanics barely graduate from high school, let alone college."

Felipe was recruited by the insurance company during his last year at Harvard. After he'd been working at his job for several years, he happened to learn that the man who recruited him was in charge of the organization's efforts to bring more minorities to the firm.

"I was stunned," Felipe remembers. "All of a sudden I was flooded with self-doubt. Maybe the people at the job who doubted my qualifications were right. Maybe I *was* only hired because I am Hispanic.

"I was terribly upset. So I went into my boss's office to talk about it. I asked him what the real situation was, and he looked at me as if I had two heads. 'They gave you an opportunity to interview here,' he explained. 'If you weren't qualified, you wouldn't be here. It's as simple as that.' He made me feel a lot better about the situation, but it really stuck with me."

> You have to believe in yourself and your accomplishments. Remember, even if no one in your family has a formal education, this does not make them ignorant or uninformed. Latinos have lacked opportunity, not intelligence. Be proud of who you—and your family—are.

2. *We are poor.* Many people have never interacted with middle-class, educated Latinos. So they tend to think of all Hispanics as the working poor—dishwashers, busboys, maids, gardeners, migrant farm workers. This image is strongly reinforced by the mainstream media, which focus a lot more attention on illegal immigrants from south of the border than on Latino contributions to the U.S. economy.

In this country, being poor is equated with a lack of initiative: it means you're lazy. The unspoken belief is that Latinos are underachievers—that even if we dress right, have the right degrees, and speak properly, we're still never going to make much of ourselves.

Carmen is a high-ranking salesperson at a national distribution company. She has a staff of more than ten people and is in line for a major promotion. Yet even her success is no protection against cultural misperceptions.

"I am not like what most people imagine a typical Latina to be," she explains. "So sometimes when I introduce myself, they're caught off guard. They seem amazed that I speak English perfectly and not with a Spanish accent.

"One Christmas I baked cookies and brought them to the office," Carmen continues. "A bunch of people gathered in the conference room for an informal party, and I heard a man from another department ask, 'Who made these cookies? They're really good.' A woman answered, 'Carmen did. She works for Joe.' And he answered, 'Gee, that was really nice of Joe to have his maid make cookies for us.'

"I was devastated by his comment. I was also angry. He just assumed that if a woman's name is Carmen, she must be a maid. When I told a non-Latino friend the story, she said I was being overly sensitive. I understand that this man was probably speaking out of his own ignorance. All he knows of Latinos is what he sees on TV, where every maid is called Maria or Carmen or Lupe. But it still hurts. I've worked so hard to get where I am, yet I realized there were still so many more obstacles ahead of me.

"Eventually I forgave the man who made the remark about my name. He didn't ask for forgiveness, but I forgave him in my heart. You can't get ahead if you carry around your anger."

> **You cannot let other people's cultural stereotypes make you bitter or resentful. You must be able to deal with a certain degree of ignorance about our culture in order to succeed in your chosen career. Your success will prove the prejudices wrong.**

3. *We are foreign.* Fred is a junior executive at a real estate company in Los Angeles. He is a third-generation Mexican American. "Last November, I was sitting around with some colleagues who were discussing their plans for Thanksgiving," he says. "One of them turned to me and said, 'I guess you won't be celebrating. Thanksgiving is an American holiday.' I politely told them that my grandmother holds a huge dinner for the entire family on Thanksgiving. I tried not to sound defensive, but I was really offended by their view of me as a 'non-American.' "

Even though Hispanics have been part of the United States since its inception, there is a perception that our loyalties lie with some foreign entity. There are many Latinos—from the second, third, and fourth generations—who have absolutely *no* ties with any country other than the United States but are still viewed in the workplace as foreign.

Often this notion is accompanied by the expectation that English is a second language for Latinos and that we are not very fluent in it. Julio's story is fairly typical. He had been flown to a midwestern city to interview for a middle-management position with a major multinational holding company. Julio thought the interview went pretty well. Apparently so did the executive with whom he had been speaking.

"You're very articulate for a Hispanic," he said to Julio, attempting to pay him a compliment, as they were finishing up. "Thank you very much," Julio responded, shaking the man's hand in the proper corporate manner. But to himself he said: "Hey, deed ju 'spec me to tal' li' dis?"

Many people are surprised that Latinos speak English fluently, articulately, and without an accent.

Your business English—both written and spoken—must be perfect.

You don't have room for mistakes, because they will be interpreted as meaning that you are not quite a "real" American.

4. *We are too family-oriented.* There is an interesting double standard in this stereotype: There is a lot of talk in this country about the importance of stressing the family and family values. Yet Hispanics are perceived as being *too* connected to their families— both immediate and extended—to make loyal managers.

Joaquín was in line for a major promotion. In charge of his company's San Antonio branch, he was being considered for the position of manager of the Columbus, Ohio, home office. During the final round of interviews, he was asked how he felt about transplanting his family from their native Texas to the Midwest. Right away Joaquín saw that his superiors were worried that he might be having doubts about moving away from a city where there was a strong Latino community to one where Hispanics were a definite minority.

"I see this as a growth opportunity for both me and *my family*," he emphasized. "I think it is important for my children to learn about another part of the country and to be exposed to new things."

Needless to say, Joaquín got the promotion. The reality is that if you refuse a transfer because you are not willing to leave your extended family or displace your children and spouse, you may not be able to make the climb up the corporate ladder.

> The stereotype persists that our strong attachment to family
> will affect our mobility. If you plan to make a career in corpo-
> rate America, you must weigh how it will affect your family.
> You must be willing to blend your values with those of the
> company you are joining.

5. *Other stereotypes.* In speaking to various groups throughout
the country about cultural and workforce diversity, these are some
of the more common stereotypes I hear about Latinos:

- We're hot-tempered.
- We're hot-blooded.
- We're quiet.
- We're shy.
- We're reserved.
- We're unorganized.
- We're always late.
- We like to cluster.
- We love to party.

> Every group is labeled with its own stereotypes. It is our
> responsibility, through our actions and successes, to change
> the preconceived notions and assumptions about Latino cul-
> ture. It is up to you to make people see you for who you are
> and who you want to be.

COUNTERACTING THE STEREOTYPE

Stereotypes obscure people's ability to see you as an individual. If
you come from a community that is considered poor and uneducated, for instance, chances are that you will be seen by some in the
same light—until you show them otherwise.

One of the challenges that Latinos face in the corporate world is the need to educate those around them to view them as individuals.

> **You want to be evaluated and promoted on your merits, and you don't want stereotypes to prevent you from being rewarded for your performance and contribution to the organization.**

The truth is, though, that we *are* products of our cultural upbringing, and we may act in certain ways that are perfectly acceptable in our community but are not appropriate in a business setting. To counteract stereotypes, you must learn to blend your actions and values into the existing corporate culture.

Dress

In the corporate environment, choice of clothing is extremely important and tends to carry a cultural meaning. A Hispanic woman wearing a vibrantly colored dress, for example, or a Latino executive sporting a gold bracelet may elicit certain ethnic associations.

Every corporation and every industry has its own dress code.

> **The smart thing to do is to read the environment and to blend in. You want to send the message that you are part of the team, that you fit. So pattern your appearance and behavior on that of the successful managers in the company.**

Style and taste in clothing are influenced by our background and culture. Imagine your best clothes when you were growing up. Remember the different set for each occasion—school clothes, play clothes, Sunday clothes, and party clothes. Now imagine a Latino who has not been exposed to corporate attire trying to decide what to wear on the first day at a new job. He might want to wear his best clothes to impress everyone, but if he shows up in his party outfit, he will be dressed inappropriately.

First you have to educate yourself about what's proper business attire for the industry you are entering. You can get advice from other people; you can go to a wardrobe consultant; you can get help from a salesperson in a clothing store.

> **First impressions are the ones that last, and you get only one chance to make a first impression.**

"I remember going for my first interview at a major publisher and not having a clue about what to wear," says Rosa, now a top editor. "My parents worked in a factory, and I didn't know anyone who worked in a job outside my neighborhood. I went into a dress store that specialized in conservative clothes and told the saleswoman what my situation was. She literally dressed me from top to bottom. Since then, I've developed my own sense of style appropriate for the workplace, but then I had no idea about the difference between 'good' clothes and 'workplace' clothes."

How you dress can also trigger other stereotypes about Latinos. In the television show "Miami Vice," for example, all the Hispanic men wore flashy suits, with open shirt collars and a lot of jewelry—clothing associated with drug dealers. So if a Latino shows up in a corporate setting wearing anything that conjures up that image, he runs the risk of being suspected of being involved in something shady or of being one of those Latin lover types. A woman who dresses with too much flash might be thought to be too sexy or even loose.

Conservative clothes imply that you will fit in, that you're willing to play by the rules. If you're perceived as having too much flash, it will be assumed that you must not have a lot of substance.

Your clothes should always blend in with your environment, so that you gain visual acceptance. The people who run your organization must think: "This person looks like me, talks like me, acts like me."

> **You must play to top management's comfort zone. You want them to look at your work, not your outfit.**

Time Relationship

Probably the most prevalent stereotype of Hispanics is that we are on cruise control and do not value time. This is particularly damaging in the business world, where time is treated as a precious commodity.

Edgar Schein, an authority on organizational culture and leadership, says that the perception and experience of time are among the most central aspects of how any group defines functions.

> **You have to respect the emphasis that the corporate culture places on time—your time, your customer's time, your boss's time, your company's time.**

When a Latino shows up to a business meeting behind schedule, he is considered to be unreliable and to have a *mañana* attitude toward his work. If a Latina comes to the office late, it is assumed that she is having family problems. The stereotypes are firmly in place, and we have to try hard to disprove them.

Luis, a Cuban American, grew up in Miami. Occasionally he would travel to New York to visit his family, but he never really considered living anyplace other than southern Florida. It was therefore a shock to his family and friends—and quite frankly to him as well—that he accepted a transfer to the Great Lakes region. He wasn't too excited about the location; after all, he was accustomed to beach weather year-round.

The transfer was necessary, however, for his career. It was a challenging assignment with great potential. The job provided the necessary exposure and access to top management. Also, if Luis was successful there, in less than three years he would be reassigned to a higher position within the organization. All things considered, a little cold weather seemed like a fair price to pay.

The first snowstorm was a brutal one. It came down all night. Luis was taken by the unfamiliar beauty of the snow. Even as he shoveled his driveway the next morning, he marveled at the splendor and novelty of it.

His joy turned to anguish, though, as the thirty-minute drive to the office dragged out into almost two and one-half hours. Luis tried to comfort himself with the thought that in this type of weather everyone else's schedule would also get pushed back a couple of hours and that the 8 A.M. staff meeting would probably start at ten or later.

Boy, was he wrong. Everyone else had been at work since eight. No one talked about the weather or the commute or the traffic. All they said was, "Where have you been? You missed the meeting." Then someone commented, "What do you expect? Luis is the *mañana* man."

Luis had never before been late to a meeting. "Certainly they could understand arriving late in this weather," he thought. "And what's with this *mañana* man, anyhow? I'm Cuban. That *mañana* stuff is about the Mexicans!"

But all his coworkers knew was that they were there on time and he was not. In their part of the country, it was understood that if it snows, you leave your house early. The worse the weather, the earlier you leave.

Luis's nickname stuck. No explanations, no footnotes, just a nickname that followed him around. He was never late again; as a matter of fact, he was usually early. He excelled. He got promoted. But he was forevermore the *mañana* man.

When you show that you value time, your behavior counteracts the stereotype that Latinos are always late or that there's "Hispanic time" and "American time." Even though you might be more focused on taking the time necessary to do the job well, often the bottom line is getting it done on time. It is also important for you to understand whether your organization works on a linear time line, with targets and milestones, or considers the overall completion of the project to be most important; you need to gauge your behavior accordingly.

The corporate environment values time. The *dicho* that time is money is not a joke. It is better to be ten minutes early than one minute late. As Latinos, we must be especially careful to be prompt and reliable about time.

Communication Style

In the corporate world, language is to the point and bottom-line. Hispanics often express ourselves less directly, using more words and verbal images to communicate and connect to those around us. We sometimes view getting right to the point as being somewhat cold and formal.

In the business context, however, using too many words is perceived as being evasive or unable to communicate your ideas succinctly. It conveys a lack of organization or preparation, a disrespect of other people's time. "Just get to the point," your supervisor may think while you are talking. "You're beating around the bush."

On the other hand, if your manager speaks to you directly, you may interpret the words as insensitive and remote. He or she might say, for example, "You have a project due. How far along are you?" To you, this might sound cold, and you automatically assume that your boss is not satisfied with your progress.

Body language and gestures are also very important in communicating in the corporate environment. Direct eye contact is crucial. It indicates honesty and directness. Looking at a person when you speak is considered essential for establishing trust and confidence in business. Even though many Latinos are taught that it is discourteous to make direct eye contact with an elder or a person of authority, you will be thought of as untrustworthy or secretive if you avoid another person's gaze.

We Latinos often use our hands to emphasize a point or animate our conversation. This is considered emotional and not very corporate. Even such a slight breach of business etiquette, however, perpetuates the stereotype that we are "outsiders" who cannot fit into the corporate environment.

Latinos tend to be more physical. We often touch each other when speaking; men greet each other with an *abrazo*; women kiss upon meeting and parting. In the workplace, even a tap on the back is considered inappropriate.

> You must be aware at all times of how you carry yourself, how you use your hands, and what your body language is communicating to others. The acceptable style of communication in the corporate culture is measured and controlled, and you must adapt to conform to its conventions.

You should also remember that there is work time and play time. Latinos often like to mix the two, with the idea that work should be an enjoyable, comfortable activity that is interwoven with our social existence. The interesting paradox is that people are promoted in the corporate setting by being able to foster these very types of relationships. Even so, work is not a time for socializing.

You should build social relationships in those settings that lend themselves to mixing business with pleasure. You hear all the time about deals that are cut on the golf course or at the tennis club. As Latinos, we have an advantage here, since we function well when relating to others in a social and personal way.

> You must use your judgment, however, to choose the appropriate time and place to begin establishing personal relationships outside the office setting.

Space

The corporate culture places a very high premium on personal space.

> Although Latinos tend to move closer to each other when we talk, in professional communication there should always be an appropriate distance between two people.

You must try to avoid reinforcing the stereotype that Latinos are touchy-feely or overly emotional. By getting too close to other people while talking, you might be perceived to be invading their space. You may seem pushy or overly familiar. Or you might give the impression of being too intimate—this also makes people uncomfortable.

Latinos who work together should respect the corporate conception of space among themselves. If they are speaking in very close proximity to each other, it may appear as if they are conspiring or sharing confidential information. They might even be thought to be speaking Spanish with each other so that no one else can understand their conversation!

Certain corporate etiquettes are identical throughout the country, whether you are in Texas or New York. The business world has its own culture, with its own distinct customs and standards. You have to adapt to it and play by its set rules.

ERASING *OUR* OLD TAPES

Stereotypes cut both ways, and Hispanics in the business world must learn to deal with Latino biases about the *güeritos*—the white male majority who occupy most of the positions of power in corporate America.

> **The only way to achieve trust and understanding with your colleagues is to acknowledge your own preconceived images and beliefs.**

We have to get away from the notion that Latinos are the only ones who are the targets of stereotypes. All groups carry these labels. And we have just as many stereotypes about the white culture as they have about us. We also have stereotypes about other Latinos within our diverse community.

Some of our stereotypes about the white majority culture include:

- They are cold and insensitive.
- They are impersonal and remote.
- They value career over family.

- They are too driven and take themselves too seriously.
- They do not know how to enjoy their work.
- They are plain; they have no flavor; there is no sense of color to their lives.

If you allow these reverse stereotypes to cloud your reasoning, you will never succeed in the corporate arena.

> **You cannot acculturate into a culture you dislike and misunderstand. You must cut through the stereotypes to see where you are.**

If the values of the corporate culture don't feel right, then you should not compromise your own belief system. In our lives there are the negotiables and the nonnegotiables. Be clear on what you are willing—and not willing—to do.

> **Incorporate only those traits that are acceptable to you, because you have to live with yourself. You have to be totally comfortable with the compromises you decide to make.**

DEAL WITH IT

Stereotypes are alive and well in corporate America. Our job is to recognize them, acknowledge them, and learn how to handle them. We have to be aware that there are prejudices about the Latino culture—as a community, as a people, and as individuals. It may not be right, but it's real.

> **Stereotypes are out there. Let's deal with them. Let's learn what's behind them and what happens when they are triggered.**

The story of Daniel, the West Coast communications executive, illustrates how stereotypes can be overcome in the pursuit of a dream.

"My upbringing was very humble," he relates. "My dad worked for the civil service in a machine shop, having worked his way up from digging ditches. For him, being a machinist was a great success. He had an amazing work ethic, and he was an important role model for me.

"When I was a sophomore in high school, I began thinking that maybe I could go to college. So I made an appointment to see my guidance counselor to ask for advice. Now, at that time in my neighborhood, there were all kinds of myths about college. The first was that you had to be brilliant to get in. The second was that even if you were a real brain, you couldn't afford it because it was so expensive. So college was a faraway dream for most of us. But I dared to dream a little bit.

"I told my guidance counselor that I wanted to prepare for college and asked her if I could take some advanced courses in English and algebra. I remember her response as if it were yesterday. She looked at me and said, 'Young man, you're not college material.' Well, I knew I wasn't a straight-A student, but all my grades were respectable B's. When she told me I wasn't college material, it was as if somebody had hit me over the head and told me that I was a moron. I was crushed.

"She then told me that she wanted to put me in a vocational program so that I could learn skills where I could be a productive member of society. I said, 'No, ma'am, that's not what I want to do. I don't want to be a carpenter.' And because I was argumentative, she took me to see the principal.

"So I went into his big office, and he pointed to all the vacant land outside his window. 'Someday people are going to build houses here,' he told me. 'Do you know that carpenters make more money than I do?'

"All of a sudden I started wondering if he was right. But then I remembered I didn't want to be a carpenter. 'It's okay they make more money than you,' I told the principal, 'but I still want to go to college.' He responded that he would reconsider his decision if my parents came in to talk to him about it. I was thrilled, thinking that my parents would surely support me. 'They'll come here and they'll fight for me,' I thought.

"But the principal was much smarter than I was. He knew that the likelihood that my dad would be able to take off work to come to see him and not lose pay was probably not very great. He also knew that my parents would probably be ashamed to try to speak to him in their broken English. So he knew that wasn't going to happen, and he was right.

"I spent the rest of high school in the building trades program. To this day, I can't hammer a nail in straight. After high school, I got a job and started going to college at night. I eventually started thinking about going full-time. As luck would have it, my mom told me that one of my cousins was going to this college in south Texas and seemed to be doing okay. So I decided to go there, too.

"I needed to borrow money from the bank and made an appointment for a loan. I went the next morning at eight, but there was a sign that gave the bank's hours as 9:30 A.M. to 3:30 P.M. At nine-thirty I went up to the loan officer, who was Latino and was wearing a white shirt and a tie. I thought, 'Wow, this guy gets off at three-thirty in the afternoon, and he works in an air-conditioned office.' Right then and there I decided to major in business!

"I'll always remember my mother's going-away speech when I went off to college. She probably didn't want me to have false expectations, because in our community no one had ever gone to college before. She told me that even if I completed just one year of college, it would be fine. She was so proud when I graduated.

"To succeed with your career plans, you have to set out your goals and objectives, challenge yourself, and overcome any barriers that are placed in front of you. You will have setbacks along the way, but you can't dwell on them. In the end, if you are good and perform, you will make it—despite the stereotypes that might stand in the way. Above all, be proud of who you are and call upon the strength of your Hispanic heritage."

Like Daniel, who did not settle for less than his dream, you cannot let what other people think about our Latino background stand in the way of your goals and ambitions. It is up to all of us to negate the stereotypes and, by example, lead the way for future generations of Hispanic executives.

Stereotypes
allow us to be:

Labeled
Characterized
Categorized

Acknowledge that they exist and learn to deal with them as if your career depended on it.

If you have to ask yourself whether something you are doing is ethical or not, it probably isn't. Management is all about making decisions that will hopefully advance your company to new levels of accomplishment. Along the way, you'll find yourself having to make decisions where "the easy way out" is sometimes to compromise the values you were raised with—honesty, integrity, concern for others, hard work, and so on.

Remember that if you compromise the values you were raised with, you are no longer the person who worked hard to get to the level of management that you have reached. More important, if you compromise your values, don't expect to be able to instill those same values in your own children. There is no boundary separating personal values from business values.

—MAXIMO C. MUÑIZ, CLU, ChFC
CORPORATE VICE PRESIDENT
NEW YORK LIFE INSURANCE COMPANY

CHAPTER 4

VALUES AND PARADIGMS

YOURS, MINE, OR OURS

El que parte y reparte, le toca la mayor parte.
The one who divides keeps the largest part.

Valeria came up with a new production-process design that promised to cut costs significantly, increasing profitability by as much as 20 percent. She sent a confidential memo outlining her idea to her immediate supervisor. Enthusiastic about the concept, Valeria's boss took her out to lunch to discuss the details of the new design. Afterward he told her that he would pass her proposal along to senior management.

Within several months, after Valeria's innovation had realized a 23 percent increase in the company's profits, her boss was promoted to division director for his initiative.

"There's no such thing as a free lunch," Valeria thought with disappointment. "I should have promoted the design myself and gotten the credit I deserve."

In the Latino culture, we are taught not to call attention to ourselves or brag about our accomplishments. *El árbol maduro, el que da más fruto, es el que está más empinado. Mientras, el que no da fruto alguno siempre tiene ramas volando por el aire.* The tree that bears the most fruit is the one that is stooped down to the ground; the tree that bears no fruit is the one whose limbs are high in the air. Yet self-promotion is key to succeeding in corporate America. If you don't spread the word about your accomplishments, no one else will.

This is just one example of the essential differences between cultural paradigms that Latinos encounter in the business world. To advance your career effectively, you need to be prepared to recognize where your values differ from those of the corporate culture, make decisions about your priorities, and blend the paradigms of your Latino background and your company.

WHOSE VALUE SYSTEM DO YOU CHOOSE?

Paradigms are defined as our perception of how things should be— our view of the world. The cultural paradigms of corporate America tend to reflect the Anglo-Saxon model. As a result, Latinos who want to pursue a business career often face tough personal choices about values.

Biculturate. Acculturate. Assimilate. What value system must you adopt to succeed in the corporate environment? Only you can answer that question, because the answer depends on your priorities, beliefs, and willingness to compromise. It is essential that you make an honest assessment of the price you are willing to pay to get ahead in management.

In charting your career path, you must decide how comfortable you are with the values and paradigms of corporate America. You must look within yourself to determine if you are willing to adjust or even transform your values and paradigms to conform to the established codes and expectations of your company. You have to consider how much, if at all, you are willing to compromise if the core values of your Hispanic heritage come into conflict with the culture of your organization.

Jerry, who was born in the Dominican Republic and raised in New York City, is an executive vice president at a major investment firm. He says that the career decisions he has made over the past ten years have been greatly influenced by his Latino upbringing.

"It comes down to what you can live with as a person, bottom line," he explains. "I hear a lot about leading a dual life. It's true: I have my Hispanic self and my corporate self. But I truly believe no matter what we do, we can still be good to our people, we can still be supportive of our people, we can still fight the battles for our people by fighting our own battles.

"Competing in business is like running a marathon. You can have all the supporters in the world helping you prepare and cheering you on from the sidelines, but when the race starts it is only you who is out there competing and who will make it to the finish line. Dedication and training will make you a winner. But when you do cross the finish line, you don't say, 'Hey, this is only for me.' You celebrate your victory with your people.

"Well-meaning managers at my company have come up to me and said, 'You can either fight for your cause or take care of number one, and that's you. Make a choice.' And I sit there thinking, 'I want to do both.'

"Since I arrived in the United States at the age of eleven, I've understood that I will automatically be considered different from the moment people hear my name. Yet at work I'm accepted. I'm considered a 'safe Hispanic,' because I behave in the corporate way. Have I compromised some of my principles? The answer is yes. Sometimes I question whether I can live with the action I need to take in a particular situation. And, honestly, I wouldn't tell my mom and dad about some of the decisions that have helped me succeed in my career.

"Compromise is a tactic that will get you to the top—to a level where you are fully empowered and in control. But compromise becomes meaningful only if you try to make a difference after you yourself have succeeded. Every Hispanic striving to move up in corporate America has at one time or another felt discouraged by a friend or a family member. 'No,' they say. 'Don't go that way. Come back.'

"I have been told by some Latinos that I have sold out. This hurts, since I have also been discriminated against because I am Hispanic. Whom should I do battle with? My compromise is to educate both sides: my colleagues and the Latino community."

To compete in the business world, you must be prepared to reconcile your personal value system and cultural beliefs with the realities of the corporate environment. You must decide whether you can live with the concessions you will have to make on your way up.

For some, the answer will be a resounding yes. For others, the solution may be finding a business climate that requires fewer compromises. And still others might decide to look for a career outside of the corporate culture.

DIFFERENT GROUPS, DIFFERENT CULTURES

Every organization has its own specific culture, with beliefs and practices that reflect a certain set of values and priorities. Every person, for his or her part, brings a core set of values to business life—values that may or may not coincide with those of the organizations we join.

Corporate culture is a reflection of the leadership of each individual company. Not only do the leaders create the culture, they manage it and enforce it. As a Latino committed to a business career, you must look at who the leaders are in corporate America, study the values they hold, and learn how those values were developed.

In his book *Organizational Culture and Leadership*, Edgar Schein explains that the critical aspect of culture is that certain things in groups are shared or held in common. He describes the following categories in the business world:

1. Observed behavioral regularities—how people interact, the language they use, the customs, traditions, and rituals they employ in a wide variety of situations

2. Group norms—the standards, values, and norms that evolve in work groups, such as the tenet of a fair day's work for a fair day's pay

3. Espoused values—the group's articulated or publicly announced principles and values

4. Formal philosophy—the broad policies and ideological principles that guide a group's actions

5. Rules of the game—the implicit rules for getting along in the organization, the "ropes" that a newcomer must learn in order to be an accepted member

6. Climate—the feeling conveyed by the physical environment and the way in which members of the group interact with each other

7. Embedded skills—the special competencies that group members display in accomplishing certain tasks

8. Habits of thinking—the mental models and linguistic paradigms that guide the perceptions, thoughts, and language used by

the members of the group, typically taught to new members early on in the socialization process

9. Shared meanings—the emergent understandings that are created by group members as they interact with each other

10. "Root metaphors"—the ideas, feelings, and images groups develop to characterize themselves

You must understand that these commonalities are already in place when you enter an organization. In order to fit into your new environment, you must take on some of these behaviors.

> **You are striving to become integrated into the corporate culture—to be accepted. You must change your view of the world before you attempt to change your behavior.**

Most Hispanics are not exposed to the corporate world until they get their first job, and so they have to learn along the way. "I had never even been inside an office until I did my college internship," says Hector, a sales trainee at a pharmaceutical company. "My father worked in a factory, and that was the only 'business' setting I knew. When I started, I was shocked to find out that I would be sharing a tiny cubicle with two other people. I had just assumed from the television shows and movies I had seen that I would be in a huge corner office with windows from floor to ceiling. I was living in a dream world!

"I also remember learning about traveling on business. I was supposed to have lunch with another salesman from my company, and he called and asked me if we could have dinner instead, because he had to go to Washington, D.C., for the day. I thought, 'How cool.' To me, plane travel was going down to San Juan laden with boxes and packages and a bag full of sandwiches to see my *abuelos* for a couple of weeks. The idea of flying with nothing more than my briefcase and the newspaper seemed so exciting. Now I dread those one-day trips."

An inherent part of the culture of any organization is the philosophy that its value system is the right one, that it accurately reflects the beliefs and goals of the group. Therefore, when you first join a company, you may hear such comments as: "This is how things are done around here. There is only one way—our way. Learn it, don't change it."

Even very progressive organizations—ones where you are encouraged to be visionary, to think outside accepted boundaries, to challenge convention—allow you to question and change everything but the core corporate value system.

> **As Latinos, we bring a very different set of core values to the corporate world. Our sense of right and wrong, of what is just and fair, of how to interact with people, is a product of our upbringing in the Hispanic culture. To achieve success in business, though, you will have to blend these core values with the ones prevalent in your company.**

CORPORATE CHARACTERISTICS

Every organization has its own set of distinctive characteristics, which include:

- A common language—the communication style that exists within the organization
- Defined boundaries—the way membership is determined in the organization; who's in, and who's out
- Power and status—the pecking order and how you get, maintain, or lose power
- Rules for relationships—both written and unwritten guidelines for how people interact with each other, with the leadership structure, their peers, their staff, the opposite gender, and so on within the organization
- Reward and punishment—the way the organization deals with people who fit in and those who are considered outcasts or "not like us"

You need to examine the prevailing characteristics and paradigms of any company you would like to work for and ask some very tough questions: Do you buy into the values and the culture of the organization? Do you share the vision of the organization? Are you comfortable with the environment in the organization? Does the corporate culture conflict with your own value system?

> **A company's value system is a crucial factor in determining whether you can succeed within the organization.**

In charting your career, you have to be very clear about what you are prepared to do to reach your goal of joining top management.

- Are you ready to negotiate your value system if you have to?
- Can you reconcile the differences between your personal value system and that of the organization?
- Are you willing to compromise your values if expected to?

After answering these questions, you might find yourself saying: "Hey, I can't do this; this doesn't feel right. It goes against who I am and what I believe in." In that case, the solution may be to look for a different company to work for—one whose culture will not require you to sacrifice your core values.

You must carefully evaluate how you are going to fit in with the rest of the organization. Try to avoid getting faked out by cultural differences. For example, you might say to an interviewer that your family is very important to you. He answers that the company, too, is family-oriented, so it's no problem. "We have a picnic in the summer," he explains, "great benefits, a Christmas party that all the kids are invited to." What he doesn't explain is that the culture of the company encourages a we're-all-one-big-family attitude and requires unwavering loyalty. If you do not understand this and take the job, you will have to make choices every day between your obligations and responsibilities to both your "families."

The key to success is having your priorities straight. You have to keep your eyes open and be equipped with enough information to make decisions based on your standards and ethics. You must determine beforehand which principles will be negotiable and which you cannot compromise.

Pick your battles carefully. That is part of learning *la política* of an organization. You may find politics distasteful, but if you don't learn and play by the rules, you will not succeed. There is a sign at the entrance of an Italian restaurant in Denver, Colorado, that says: "If you don't like garlic, go home." The same is true of *la política* in corporate America.

Remember, there is no right and wrong here. It really comes down to personal integrity. Your core values and beliefs have to determine whether you continue your climb up the corporate ladder or not.

POTENTIAL AREAS OF CONFLICT

As a Hispanic, you must judge your comfort level with the values of corporate America in light of your cultural background. Some potential areas of conflict include:

- Realizing career ambitions vs. fulfilling family obligations
- Challenging authority appropriately vs. deferring to people in positions of power
- Learning to self-promote vs. stressing modesty and humility
- Blending vs. balancing

Once again, these are areas where honest introspection and self-analysis are critical.

Career Ambitions vs. Family Obligations

Latinos have always attached a special importance to family and community. Yet to advance your career, you may have to move far away from family and friends, to a part of the country where you know no one or possibly even overseas.

> **Flexibility and mobility are issues that Latino executives commonly confront.**

Many Latinos are fearful about abandoning their family structures when they choose to accept a transfer to another city. They feel that they are uprooting their spouse and children by taking them away from the support networks of extended family and friends. Yet if management perceives they are unwilling to make geographic compromises for the good of the company, their chances of moving up will quickly become nonexistent.

"When I told my mother that I had received a promotion and might be moving to Des Moines, her response was: '¿Por qué tan lejos? Why so far away?' " relates Julia, a Dallas advertising executive. "My mother doesn't understand why I would want to leave the nest. She is also concerned that there might not be a strong Latino community where I'm going. But if I want to make it in my company, I know I have to go where they send me—willingly and enthusiastically!"

In addition to being geographically mobile, Latino managers must also be flexible about being able to fulfill their personal family roles. For example, a Latina executive who is required to work weekends to complete a project or to travel for business will have less time to spend with her husband and children. Since there are firmly established female roles in the Latino culture, this is likely to create a direct conflict with some core Hispanic values. She will have to choose between what is expected of her as a traditional Latina wife and mother and the established practices of corporate America, where your work may come before your family.

"When I have to work late, my father asks, '¿Y, te pagan por eso?' He thinks it's paid overtime," says Frank, an insurance company trainee. "My mother calls me every day to ask if I'll be home for dinner. I tell her that I don't know how late I'll be, but I can't get her to understand that my long hours are not only the demands of my job, but also my choice."

You should approach your career choices as a family decision, since they will affect the whole family. Discuss and negotiate them with your spouse, your children, your parents, your partner, your extended family. Again, there is no right or wrong way to handle things, but you must be aware that the decisions you make about your professional life will have consequences in your personal life.

> **Ask for advice from your family, friends, and mentors. Consult your peers, coworkers, superiors, and subordinates within the organization. Take in all their advice, sift through it, and then make the decision that's best for you. If you do not compromise or risk your core values, your decisions will most likely lead to fulfilling success. It is therefore critical that you be clear about your priorities.**

Steven Covey, author of *The Seven Habits of Highly Effective People*, suggests formulating a personal mission statement that clarifies your goals and objectives in such areas as education; family; finances; health and fitness; and social, cultural, and spiritual life. For example, in listing your priorities, you may find that you are not willing to move your family to another city—away from their community—under any circumstances. Then, if the issue of a transfer comes up, your decision will have already been made and you don't have to go through any turmoil or self-doubt.

> **The goal is to integrate your professional and personal values and priorities so that you can lead a life that is smoothly blended, not precariously balanced.**

Challenging Authority vs. Deferring to People in Positions of Power

As Latinos, we are raised with respect for authority. *"Sea respetuoso,"* we have been told since we were young children. Yet in the corporate setting there are often occasions when we must challenge the actions or decisions of people in power.

Take the example of Jorge, a young engineer who was recently hired by an auto-parts manufacturer. Soon after starting his new job, Jorge noticed a design flaw in a brake part that was likely to compromise consumer safety. He also knew, however, that correcting the defect would involve a product recall and would significantly reduce the company's profit margin in the short term.

Jorge was faced with a dilemma: Should he come forward and alert his superiors? He realized he had to take into account several factors: the values of the company, whether it was driven exclusively by the bottom line or whether quality was also a priority, whether employees were expected to point out problems or to toe the line, and whether they would even listen to someone so new on the job.

Jorge was in a real quandary. His sense of responsibility and integrity told him that he must say something about the design flaw to his supervisors. His Latino upbringing, on the other hand, made him feel that by speaking up he would be challenging the authority of the management. Yet Latino culture also stresses doing the right thing. Jorge feared that even if he insisted that the problem must be fixed, he would be overruled and would be labeled a troublemaker, a whistle-blower, a do-gooder, a granola-eater, a tree-hugger— whatever name you want.

But ultimately Jorge had to live with himself. He decided that acting on his convictions was more important to him than fitting in. He realized that he would not want to remain at a company that valued profits over safety, and so he chose to speak up. He got advice on how to frame his finding appropriately and wrote a detailed report on the defective part, its effect on safety, and a proposed plan for correcting it. Jorge's reward for his courage was a promotion and the admiration of his coworkers and superiors.

The Latino culture is very respectful of people in positions of authority: teachers, law enforcement officers, employers, and so on. It is hierarchical, with great reverence for age. We hold our elders in high regard and are deferential with our parents and grandparents.

These traits would seem to be assets in the corporate setting. Yet in the competitive business environment, you run the risk of coming across as too meek or as an apple-polisher if you answer with, "Yes, sir; no, sir; yes, ma'am; no, ma'am." You may even be viewed as an outsider, a foreigner. By exhibiting a cultural trait that is the norm in our community, you may be stereotyped as a pushover or a brownnoser.

Another example of conflict, because of the importance put on age in our culture, is what happens when you find yourself in the position of supervising an older professional. Would you address her as "Ms. Smith"? Would you say "yes, sir" to him? No—you must learn the protocol of the corporate culture and project the appropriate image of the position you occupy.

> **It goes back to reading the environment. You must find out what the authority relationships are in your company and learn to act within those norms.**

Self-promotion vs. Humility

In the Latino culture, children are told that they're not supposed to be too conspicuous, that they shouldn't call attention to themselves. *Pórtate bien, no hagas ruido.* Because of the strong work ethic that exists in our community, the conventional wisdom is that if you do your best and are diligent in your responsibilities, your efforts will be noticed and rewarded.

In corporate America, things are very different. There is always someone who is ready to take credit for a good idea and self-promote, even at another person's expense. There is a specific structure within organizations, a defined pecking order and hierarchy. Even with the newer organizational models—flat organizations consisting of cross-functional teams—there is always a leader who stands out from the rest of the crowd. Remember, while there is no *I* in *TEAM*, there is a *ME*.

Promoting yourself is an acquired skill. It is something you learn as part of your on-the-job educational process. As you continually define and refine your professional capabilities, you will have to champion your accomplishments and let others know about your achievements. Even though we Latinos might follow the Mexican adage *"No le eches mucha crema a tus tacos,"* be careful about being too proud or boastful; it does not translate well into the corporate world.

Roberto, who works as a sales representative for a major software company, learned the hard way about the importance of tooting his own horn. "I'm Puerto Rican and the first member of my family to graduate from college," he says. "My first job in a corporation was a total culture shock. I had never been in that environment before and had to learn how to carry myself in a corporate setting. At the beginning, I was stiff and uncomfortable. I didn't understand office politics. I didn't realize how important it is whom you know, that you have to look for a person to bring you in.

"I didn't look out for myself. One day I was offered an opportunity to interview for a higher-level position that required the ability to speak Spanish. I was flattered but also mentioned that one of my coworkers spoke Spanish, too. When he ended up getting the job instead of me, I was very upset. I finally asked my boss what had happened, and he explained that the management had interpreted my answer as a lack of interest on my part. They thought that because I had recommended someone else for the job, I must not have been interested or was afraid of the increased responsibilities.

"Now I know I should have said, 'Yes, I want the job.' But the Hispanic culture is a more collective one, where we include other people. We don't just look out for ourselves, thinking we're number one and forgetting everybody else. I remember during one of my first job interviews, I was asked to describe the specifics of my previous position. I kept using the term 'we' all the time. I said, 'We did this' and 'We did that.' Finally the interviewer interrupted me. 'Yes, but what did *you* do?' she wanted to know. I was characterizing my work as part of a team effort, and she was looking for a decision maker."

One of the ways to begin to promote yourself is to seek out the help of someone who knows the ropes—a person who is part of the informal power structure. This person will probably be more comfortable with selling your talents and promoting your image than you are. He or she can assist you, mentor you, coach you, and call attention to your accomplishments.

In addition, you must get involved with high-profile projects—projects that will get you noticed and singled out. You may have to sell an idea to get assigned to a new project; you may have to develop a new product or an advertising campaign; you may have to think up a new sales strategy or promotion. There will be presentations you will have to make to senior-level executives, who will have to be convinced to buy into or endorse your ideas. Certainly there will be a reporting process to measure, monitor, and evaluate the project. Reporting usually requires a front person or spokesperson to be in charge of making presentations. *This should be you.*

There is a *dicho* in Spanish: *El que no habla, Dios no lo oye*—if you don't say anything, God won't hear you. The same is true with corporate leadership. Work to make your presence known throughout the organization.

"I volunteered for everything," says Rosario, the New York banking executive. "No matter how difficult the project was—even if I had no idea what it was about—I said, 'I'll do it, I'll do it, I'll do it.' And while a lot of my colleagues were sitting around groaning that they couldn't handle any more work, I was always raising my hand. Eventually my behavior caught the eye of senior management.

"I like being seen as a worker who is completely dependable—my supervisors know I will do whatever it takes to get the job done. It's a lot of hard work, but I'm resilient. Once you have the reputation of being dependable, you will start getting projects. Then you will begin to stand out in the crowd.

"Yet working extra hours is not enough. One of the formulas for success at a corporation is always letting your boss—and your boss's boss—know what you are doing. Hispanics are taught to be modest and respect authority. We have to erase those old tapes to get the proper credit in the workplace. If we don't take credit for our achievements, someone else will.

"You must be prepared to seize opportunities as they come along. For whatever reason, I kept driving myself to go to school. I'm not sure why I did it, but something inside told me that the way I was going to move up was to get educated, so I kept pushing myself. It was tough at times, very tough. But what it did was offer me choices. When I would come to a fork in the road, I could base my decisions on options, not necessity. I did not have to limit myself. Being prepared is a very important key to success. You may not know exactly what will happen down the road, but you know you'll be ready for whatever comes your way."

In the Hispanic culture, children are taught to be well behaved, quiet, and polite. The reality is, though, that you don't get ahead if you are invisible, no matter how well behaved you are. Think back to when you were in grade school. Who got all the attention? You remember: "Billy's so smart. Billy's so interested in everything." Well, Billy was the kid who was always ready with his hand up in the air when the teacher asked a question. Sometimes the Latino students were waiting meekly to be called on. And you probably knew the correct answer!

"Corporate America doesn't understand the Latino culture," observes Hernán, a manager in the aerospace industry. "They don't understand who we are. For example, when we go on an interview, we find it very difficult to expound on our accomplishments, because we're a very humble people.

"A Latina had applied for a job as an assistant in the sales department at my company. The man who interviewed her told me he had been turned off by her emphasizing the fact that she had gone back to college after several years of working as a secretary. 'Why did she keep mentioning this?' he asked me. 'Doesn't that sound defensive to you?' I explained to him that in the Hispanic culture completing one's education is considered a tremendous achievement and she was proud about what she had done.

"Afterward I thought how helpful it would have been if another Hispanic had been sitting in on the interview. We could have acknowledged the fact that pursuing your degree is a big thing and tried to explain its importance to her potential boss. There is a wide gap between how Anglo Americans perceive Latinos and what they understand about us. There are many cultural pieces that have not yet come together."

> In the corporate arena, if you do your work diligently but never raise your hand, so to speak, you will quickly be labeled a good back-room worker. You will not be promoted, because you will not be demonstrating the leadership qualities that are necessary to rise in management.

Blending vs. Balancing

For most of us who have to make a living and provide for our families, the model has always been to attempt to achieve a balance between our professional and personal lives. Such a balancing act is extremely hard to pull off, however. We try to juggle all of our various responsibilities but invariably drop something and end up having to pick up the pieces.

There is an alternative. If you have satisfying, rewarding, and enjoyable professional and personal lives, why not try to blend them? Why not begin to incorporate your family into your work and your professional life into your home?

Let's say you have a business trip scheduled for the weekend your son is turning nine. Under the balancing model, you would either have to disappoint your son by being away or jeopardize your standing at work by turning down the assignment. One way or the other, you would have to say no to someone.

Under the blending model, your family is very much aware of the work you do. You share with them how important your job is to you and how it fits into your life and the life of the family. The weekend assignment, in this scenario, is an opportunity to incorporate your son into your professional life by bringing him along on your business trip. You would be exposing him to your work while at the same time building a family event around required business travel. Involving children in our professional lives is the premise behind Take Our Daughters to Work Day (now called Take Our Children to Work Day, because boys are also included).

To blend successfully, you must look for employment in an organization that is compatible with your values. If your company frowns on mixing work with family, you will find yourself struggling with an essential incompatibility. And, once again, you will be forced to do the balancing act.

Your social and civic interests can also be incorporated into the blending model. If you're an individual who feels a responsibility to your community, you might want to get involved in an inner-city sports league or youth mentorship program, for example. Instead of having to choose community involvement and interest in social causes over the obligations of your job, you can use your professional accomplishments to help others.

In order to blend well, you must be honest about your core values. You have to know who you are and what drives you. You have to determine how much you are willing to compromise. It's what I call the "pucker factor," a picture of someone puckering up and saying, "Ooh, I can't do that."

To begin, write down what is important to you. Then list the issues you feel strongly about—those you know you won't budge on. Share these resolutions with the family members and friends closest to you, who understand and know you. Show the list to people who will be honest with you, who will call you on it if they see at a future date that you are compromising one of the items you claim is important to you.

"Latinos have a wide range—we're not one-dimensional," says Henry, a telecommunications executive. "But to make it, we must mainstream first. As we feel more secure and achieve a greater level of success in our careers, we can embrace our Hispanic heritage more openly. For example, when I first started at the company, I would not serve my boss Latino food when I invited him over to my house for dinner. Now when he comes, I serve *arroz con pollo* and put on salsa music. And he loves it!

"I believe Latinos can fit into both cultures without being defined by either. We should use our background to our advantage. The Latino culture is very social, for example, and it helps us form interpersonal relationships at work. We are a diverse people, and this makes us more flexible and open. We can adapt to our company's culture. I'm extremely suspicious of people who make themselves one-dimensional, whether they're Latino or white. It's one thing to be proud of your culture and who you are; it's another thing to decide that the rest of the world doesn't matter.

"Latinos have a great advantage in the corporate world. Depending on the situation, we can adapt and act different ways. If we're in corporate America, we behave like corporate America. In our community, we can reconnect to our Hispanic roots. We can get much further this way than if we limit ourselves to a strict Latino environment or a strict corporate environment. It's very important to use this duality to our advantage."

The Latino culture is rich with diverse people and traditions. Use this to your advantage in adapting to your work environment. Blend your professional and personal lives to create a new culture that combines the best of both worlds.

CONSTANT REASSESSMENT

You should be constantly reassessing your priorities and how well they conform to the value system of your organization. Make an effort to distinguish between core values and stereotypes. You may have to discard some of your preconceived notions and replace them with other images. To do so, you must be open, communicative, and reach out to learn more about other people. If you are comfortable with who you are, you will be only refining your priorities, not changing your basic value system.

> Only you can judge your comfort level with the values and paradigms of corporate America. You have to decide if you are willing to make concessions with the core values of your Hispanic culture if they conflict with those of your business environment. Look inside yourself to see if you can accommodate, negotiate, and resolve differences in order to succeed in your professional career.

**Every organization
has a culture.**

Every people has a culture.

**How well you understand yours
and theirs will determine the
extent to which there is
comfort and *fit*.**

Many young Latinos don't understand the critical importance of a mentor until they are "wounded" and need a "guardian angel" to defend their character, capabilities, or future potential to others. Looking for one at that point is too late. A good "guardian angel" would have already planted the seeds of a positive impression all around. Then when the inevitable slipup happens (part of every person's career, no matter how bright or successful he/she is), these individuals can overcome the hurdle at least as well if not better than their colleagues— and will have a respected person there to coach them so they don't repeat the error. Like Yoda in Star Wars and Glenda the Good Witch in The Wizard of Oz, mentors don't prevent the precious learning experience that comes from a fall— but they are there to pick you up, dust you off, and tell you to keep moving forward.

—MARIA E. ALVAREZ
VICE PRESIDENT
CHASE MANHATTAN BANK, N.A.

CHAPTER 5

WHAT YOU DON'T KNOW AND THEY WON'T TELL YOU

The Rules Mamá Never Taught You

Ojos que no ven, corazón que no siente.
What you don't see or know won't hurt you. (Wrong!)

Lloyd, a senior partner at a major investment firm, and his wife are preparing to host a dinner party for his business associates and clients. Lloyd, who is white, received his undergraduate degree from Princeton and his MBA from Harvard. He has been recently elected president of the board of trustees of his country club.

Before the guests arrive, Lloyd calls his young son over for a chat. "I want you to introduce yourself to all the people in the room," he instructs the boy. "Stride right up to each one of them, look them straight in the eye, stretch out your arm, and give them a good firm handshake. Then say your name and welcome them to our home."

Lloyd has just given his son a lesson in social graces and business etiquette. He has also done some powerful grooming for the executive suite.

For Javier, a high-school science teacher of Mexican descent, the preceding scenario would present some conflict. The Latino culture places a high value on honoring elders and those in positions of authority. Therefore, Javier has taught his young son to wait to be introduced and addressed by an adult before speaking up. In addition, because it might be considered discourteous—and possibly even challenging—for a Hispanic youngster to look a grown-up he doesn't know square in the eye, Javier's son might look away or even glance downward as a way of showing respect to his father's guests.

Imagine these two youngsters twenty years later. Give them equal education and work experience. In a corporate setting, it is Lloyd's son who has the clear advantage. He will confidently walk up to his supervisors and introduce himself without waiting to be called on. He will be perceived by the company leadership as outgoing, confident, and assertive. He will be regarded as a person who fits in and reflects the company's image.

If Javier's son hasn't picked up these skills during his school years, he is at a distinct disadvantage. If he has not learned the art of studied informality and the value of eye contact, his supervisors might judge him to be shifty, up to something, or too unpolished for the social requirements of the job. Javier's son might also be regarded as too meek or passive if he is overly deferential to people in positions of authority, addressing his supervisors as "sir" or "ma'am" to show respect. Following the social rules of his Latino culture rather than those accepted in the corporate world will eliminate Javier's son from consideration for high-profile work assignments and eventual advancement into the upper levels of management.

WAKE-UP CALL

To compete in today's business environment, you must learn the rules of the game in the corporate arena. These are the unwritten protocols and unspoken subtleties we Latinos do not learn from our *mamás*. These are lessons we were never taught in school.

For example, I recently had the opportunity to spend some time on the road with the president of a major corporation. At one of his presentations, he took some lighthearted jabs at me. Later he asked me to address a gathering of all the employees at the corporate office. He explained that in an effort to boost morale, he wanted me to prepare a roast of the senior management and make it as irreverent as possible.

Remembering the shots he had taken at me, I took special joy in poking fun at him and his staff. The roast was a huge success. The employees were able to have a laugh at the expense of their leaders, and the executives ate up the attention.

Even though I thoroughly enjoyed myself and knew I had contributed to improving the company's morale, I was also aware that I had broken every rule my parents ever taught me regarding respecting authority and deferring to people in positions of power. "What would my mother and father say about what I've done?" I asked myself. One day I decided to find out, and I told them how I had made fun of the bosses during the company roast.

Not surprisingly, my parents were disappointed and shocked. "Is this how we brought you up?" my mother wanted to know. "Is this what we taught you?" my father asked. I smiled to myself and thought, "Fortunately, I picked up this little bit of corporate etiquette on my own."

To be welcomed into the informal network within your company that leads to the inner circle of decision making and power, you must break through the cultural barriers—your own and other people's—that stand in the way of advancement.

> **If you want to crash through the glass ceiling that keeps Latinos from moving beyond a certain level of responsibility in corporate America, you have to wake up to the fact that no matter how excellent your credentials or how sharp your skills, your success will be decided by how well you fit into the corporate culture.**

More Latinos than ever before are now entering the business world. Yet even with our college degrees and MBAs, we are an unknown for most companies. In interviews, you will be evaluated not only in terms of technical and intellectual abilities but also in terms of *comfort* and *fit*: How well will you get along in the company? Will you click? Are you comfortable with the corporate environment? Do others feel comfortable around you? How good are your interpersonal skills? Can you be a team player?

Most Latinos learn of employment opportunities through career counselors and job postings. *Nuestros padres* are not part of the social set where the majority of executives *se andan codeando*, rub elbows. We are not members of the same civic and recreational groups as our future employers. We are not plugged into the system of informal networks where available jobs are casually mentioned and suggestions for suitable candidates often solicited. *Acuérdate, eres* outsider *aquí*.

As a result, most Latinos start out cold in the search for entry into the corporate world. Your first interview at the company where you want to work will most likely be with a representative from the human resources department. Although the human resources person will make the crucial decision whether or not your educational credentials, technical skills, and work experience are a good match for the organization, this person will ultimately have nothing to do with your career path. It is strictly his or her job to decide if you qualify for the crucial interview with the manager who is hiring. This second interview will be the initial test of how familiar you are with the rules that govern behavior in the corporate world.

RULE ONE: BEYOND THE HUMAN RESOURCES DEPARTMENT, IT IS NOT WHAT YOU KNOW BUT WHO YOU ARE THAT REALLY MATTERS

Ester, a recent graduate of the University of Miami, is excited about the possibility of working in the marketing department of a major airline. She calls her brother, Rogelio, bursting with optimism.

"I got called back for a second interview," she tells him. "I think I got the job. Why else would they invite me back?"

"Ay, Ester, wake up and smell the *atole, hermana,*" he replies. "All that means is that you have good grades, you have some experience, and you were *educada,* polite, in the interview. Good grades, respect, and charm might have worked to get money and gifts out of *Tía* Chela, but it's going to take more than that to land this job."

In school, you are told that it is important to emphasize to potential employers that you're well rounded—a Renaissance person. It goes without saying that you should underscore your educational accomplishments and past work experience. Yet once you clear the hurdle of the initial interview, you must keep in mind that you will have to do a different kind of selling to land the job.

> **Once your competence has been established, it is up to you to demonstrate that you will fit into the company and be part of the team.**

The human resources representative decides if your background and skills make you a viable candidate for the job. In Ester's case, for example, the personnel office decided that she has the education, intelligence, and experience to qualify for a second interview.

Now Ester will meet with the vice president of marketing, whose job it is to evaluate whether she will fit into the organization. She will judge whether Ester will blend in with the climate of the company, what kind of player she'll be on the team, and whether she has the capacity to lead others and be respected by them.

If Ester goes into this interview thinking she is being evaluated in terms of what she knows rather than who she is, chances are she and the interviewer will be talking at cross purposes.

"I never thought I would be offered the position," says Rosario, the banking executive from New York, recalling her first job interview for a summer internship during business school. "The work was in the treasury area of a bank, something I had no experience in. All the descriptions and talk were going completely over my head. I remember sitting there, telling myself just to be pleasant in order to make it through the interview. When they called to say I was hired, I was really surprised. How had I impressed my future boss? What in the world did he possibly see in me?

"After several weeks on the job, I worked up the nerve to ask my boss why he had chosen me. He laughed and said, 'I could see by your résumé and educational background that you were intelligent. But during the interview, I knew you were smart enough to understand what was expected of you. I also picked up that you would make a good team player. It was my intuition, something I could only know from speaking to you in person. There's a certain click between two people that occurs in an interview, and we had it.' "

There is a big difference between being sponsored or networked into a job and applying without knowing anyone in the organization. An executive who learns that a friend's son is graduating from business school and looking for work might set up an interview with the young man directly. Because there is an established family or business connection, it is assumed that the candidate's background will be compatible with that of others in the company.

In this case, the interview process is reversed. The meeting with the representative of the human resources department will be the last formality in the hiring process.

The *bond* between the executive and the candidate is already in place—their meeting will just serve to secure it.

To maximize your chances of getting hired, you must learn as much as possible about the organization before you go to your first interview: what the environment of the company is like, the mood of the place, its specific culture, how the people look and act and speak. *Entiéndalo tú*—figure it out. You get the message.

> **If you aren't adequately prepared, you'll find yourself dancing a merengue to rock music. The interview will be a disaster. You will be giving great answers to the wrong questions. You will be engaged in a two-way monologue.**

Even if you have learned the appropriate rules and etiquette from reading books and taking business courses, there is no substitute for being directly exposed to corporate culture and experiencing it firsthand. It's like finding yourself in Paris with three years of high school French under your belt. The first thing you realize is that you don't know how to find the rest room. You've spent three years learning things that have little or no practical application.

> **There are nuances and subtleties that can be picked up only by *being* there.**

As a Hispanic, how can you possibly compete in the corporate world if you lack this kind of exposure? How can you prepare yourself to convince the vice president that you are the right fit for the job? How can you ready yourself to ease into the structure of the organization as smoothly as possible?

First of all, look for the opportunities to get in there and play! Make a plan to enter the competition *para que luzcas*, so you'll be noticed:

- Seek out internships while you are in school to become exposed to the world of business and management. Submerge yourself in the corporate culture. Watch what everyone else does. Observe and incorporate.
- If you are no longer a student, look for networking opportunities. There is a variety of Latino professional associations, business alliances, and ethnic organizations you might want to join. Use these groups to meet other Latinos in the corporate arena and start creating your own network.

- Find Latino executives who have become "insiders." *Sabe más el diablo por viejo que por diablo.* The devil is smart because he's experienced, not because he's the devil. Learn from those who have been around and have paid their dues. Always be ready to learn—absorb everything you can. Pay special attention to what influential Hispanic managers have done to achieve access within their companies.
- Identify role models. You are never too old to look for guidance and advice. Don't limit yourself only to Latinos; look for men and women who have made it in the industry or field you wish to enter.
- Set up informational meetings with successful managers and executives. Interview them, get tips based on their inside experience, ask for names of people who might be looking to hire. Think of your career as an enterprise. You need a board of directors—this is the core of your network.

Getting your foot in the door of a corporation is an education in itself. Do not allow your Hispanic identity to define or confine how you are viewed by others. Be fully prepared when you start work. Know that you're qualified to do your job. Act confident and secure. Communicate, beyond a doubt, that you are comfortable with the organizational structure of the company; that this is a good match; that you are the right person for the position.

RULE TWO: GETTING HIRED DOESN'T NECESSARILY MAKE YOU A PLAYER

Being picked for the job does not automatically guarantee a place on the team. As soon as you start work it is up to you to show your supervisors that you are qualified to be a player. You must demonstrate that you will be able to handle high-profile assignments that ensure exposure and recognition. How? Don't be afraid to show you are smart, that you are hungry to do the work, and that you fit comfortably into the existing corporate environment.

You might be one of the first Latinos your supervisors know in a business or social setting. They may feel uncomfortable with some of the differences—real or perceived—between the Hispanic culture and their own. They might already expect you to act in a certain way. It is up to you to lay these stereotypes to rest, to understand that certain assumptions might be made about you because of people's unfamiliarity with your Hispanic heritage.

It is essential to keep in mind that your performance will be evaluated after you have held the job for a while to determine your future with the company. You will be judged on how well you are doing your job; how you get along with your peers and supervisors; your potential to lead and command respect; and, most important, how you reflect and exemplify the image the corporation wants to project to the rest of the world.

Your goal is to be selected for the team—and for a crucial position on that team. You want to be brought along and helped up the corporate ladder. To accomplish this, you must first be recognized for doing your work well. Second, you have to demonstrate your ability to blend in, to assimilate your Hispanic upbringing with the culture of your workplace. You must understand and be at ease in your environment. Finally, you need to seek out a senior manager who is willing to be your guide.

Breaking into the upper levels of management requires coaching, mentoring, and sponsorship by those already in positions of power. Someone high up in the company hierarchy must be comfortable enough with you—have enough *confianza*—to tell you what and what not to do, what is considered acceptable and what is not. The goal is to have this person eventually say to his fellow executives, "Hey, I'm bringing this one up."

This is where cultural stereotypes about Latinos can be a real stumbling block.

> Be practical, but remember: Make it *your* responsibility to make your supervisors comfortable with you, not the other way around.

RULE THREE: BE AWARE OF CULTURAL STEREOTYPING

Ninety-seven percent of senior-management jobs in the United States are held by white men, according to the 1990 census. In a survey conducted by the Hispanic Policy Development Project in 1994, the majority of these executives indicated that they were not comfortable with what they perceived as Hispanic differences—or what they *expected* might be unfamiliar about the Latinos with whom they worked—even when no differences were immediately evident.

This expressed discomfort often translates into a reluctance to sponsor and mentor Hispanic men and women into positions of power and responsibility within corporations. For the Latino who is looking to rise in management, to be excluded from the informal communication network of the company means to be denied access to the high-profile assignments that provide essential visibility.

What can you do to cure ethnic stereotyping? Maybe nothing. Why? Because you are working with other people's *equipaje*, baggage—their hang-ups. You can spend a lot of time and energy trying to change something over which you have little or no control. Don't use up your energy this way.

Sidestep the negativity, or else you will succumb to it. A better approach is to try to preempt stereotyping. *El que pega primero pega dos veces*. Be empathetic, acknowledge the fears, and then put them to rest.

"I know you've never had another Latino manager here," you can say to your boss. "You may have a concern as to how I'll fit in.

Let me assure you that I have excellent skills in dealing with nonethnic situations."

> **Accept that cultural stereotypes and preconceptions exist and that they will impact your career. Make sure you understand what these stereotypes are, what expectations they trigger, and how they may affect you.**

RULE FOUR: YOU DON'T HAVE TO EXHIBIT A PARTICULAR TRAIT TO BE STEREOTYPED

Our values and behavior are defined by the different cultures to which we belong—whether it be Hispanic, white, corporate, or any other. Since our values are formulated at an early age, we bring our baggage of preconceived notions and images with us wherever we go.

As a Hispanic striving to make it in the corporate environment, you will have certain doubts and apprehensions about your colleagues and your supervisors. "They're uncomfortable with me because I'm Latino," you may think. "They don't know what to say to me. They've never worked with a Latino before. They don't understand my values. And I don't understand theirs."

Some Latinos are considered "safe." Our skin color, the way we speak, and the degree to which we've assimilated into the mainstream culture make us seem part of white America. The rest of us, however, must be aware that our cultural traits and physical attributes automatically set off certain associations and assumptions.

As you begin moving ahead in your career, you should keep in mind that there will always be stereotypes that will make others cautious of you, and you of them. Even if these seem unfair—or even discriminatory—you must be ready to acknowledge and address them in order to advance in corporate America.

RULE FIVE: RECOGNIZE THE CULTURAL STEREOTYPES THAT MIGHT AFFECT COMMUNICATION

Sofía gets stuck in an early-morning traffic jam and is five minutes late to her department's weekly sales meeting. As she slips into the conference room she catches her boss looking disapprovingly at his watch. She's unsure if his displeasure is based on the fact that she was late this one time or if he is really thinking, "You can't trust Puerto Ricans to be on time." Sofía makes a vow to be ten minutes early to all future meetings and appointments.

Latinos in the corporate world encounter a variety of broad stereotypes on a daily basis. According to the Glass Ceiling Commission's 1991 study of the barriers faced by women and ethnic and racial groups in corporate America, preconceived notions about Latinos often negatively impact our potential to be considered as candidates for corporate leadership.

The commission reported that commonly held stereotypes about Latinos include the following:

- Hispanics have a *mañana* attitude—are laid back and attuned to a slower pace, and do not consider time to be of the essence.
- Hispanics place family obligations before work commitments.
- They are more loyal to fellow Latinos than to others in the organization.
- They are unable to perform certain jobs because of a lack of exposure or familiarity.

It is up to you, as a Latino employee, to counteract these stereotypes by blending in with the accepted norms of your organization's corporate culture. Preconceptions can limit you only if you validate them through your actions.

RULE SIX: LEARN TO READ THE CORPORATE ENVIRONMENT

My cousin Fernando was doing graduate work in accounting at a major university. It was the policy of the accounting faculty to require degree candidates to wear business attire for their oral examinations. Fernando wasn't concerned because he always considered himself a fashion statement.

When my cousin appeared for his exam, his professor took one look at him and said: "Mr. Melendez, rock stars have a manner of dress, bullfighters have a manner of dress, business executives have a manner of dress. You, sir, have come dressed as either a bullfighter or a rock star, but nothing like an executive."

As I crisscross the country giving seminars and workshops for Hispanic managers and executives, and students looking to climb the corporate ladder, the most common question I am asked is: How can I be accepted within my organization and move beyond my present position?

The answer is simple: *Abra los ojos y aprenda.*

> **You must learn to become part of the defined culture of your company, so that those in positions of power will be comfortable with you and be willing to mentor you into senior management.**

Culture is defined as a shared set of beliefs, customs, values, language, and traditions. If we are determined to succeed in our careers, it is up to us to understand the culture of our workplace and adjust our conduct accordingly.

> **Fit, fit, fit, fit. People feel best with people who look like them, think like them, speak like them, and act like them.**

To begin, study the environment around you. Every company has its own image. It is very different working in a major Wall

Street law firm, a high-tech software company, an investment bank, or a major Hollywood studio. Observe how people dress, what kind of accessories they wear, the briefcases they carry, the writing instruments they own, how they decorate their offices, their manner of speaking, their body language. Learn what professional organizations they belong to, their recreational interests, the charities they support.

If you have been exposed to the business world through your parents or background, you probably have a feel for these cultural nuances. Most Latinos, however, don't have the benefit of having grown up in professional circles and will have to acquire these skills on the job.

How do you learn these skills? Most important is to find a sponsor to help you understand the subtle details of your organization that cannot be picked up by observation alone. But what can you do to attract a potential mentor? How can you interest a senior executive in your career and have him or her help you join upper management?

First, let it be known that you want to move up the corporate ladder, *que quieres avanzar*. Communicate your willingness to blend into the existing environment in order to get ahead. Next, demonstrate a desire to be coached along, to be guided and directed. Make sure you show your loyalty to the organization and to your potential mentor. Finally, get involved in civic and social activities that will afford you the chance to meet your company's top managers in a nonbusiness setting.

At this point, you must step back and honestly assess your present standing in the organization. Ask yourself the following questions:

PERFORMANCE

1. Am I cutting it? Does the quality of my work exceed the standards of my company?

2. Do I initiate work, or do I wait for assignments?

3. Do I meet deadlines? Am I dependable?

4. Am I a team player? Am I respected by my peers?

5. Am I a leader?

6. Am I willing to give my all for the company?

IMAGE

1. Does my image match my position? Do I look and act the part?

2. Am I aware of the nonverbal cues, such as grooming, clothes, and accessories, that are considered important in my company?

3. Does my body language reflect self-assurance? Is my handshake firm, my posture erect, my eye contact direct?

4. How do I speak? Is my grammar correct? My pronunciation? How familiar am I with the technical language in my industry?

5. What is my demeanor? Do I carry myself with confidence and pride?

6. Will a senior executive trust me enough to stand in front of his or her colleagues, supervisors, board, or stockholders and say about me, "This is my choice"?

PROFILE

1. What is the level of my exposure in the company?

2. Do I get high-profile assignments?

3. Do I get proper credit for my work?

4. Are my accomplishments noticed by my supervisors?

5. Am I decisive and willing to take charge?

6. Can I question authority in an appropriate manner, or am I too passive?

7. Do I carefully weigh all the considerations before I take action?

8. Am I able to promote myself, or do I feel that by talking about my achievements I am bragging?

> **You don't get ahead by accident. Success is planned—by you and for you.**

RULE SEVEN: BEGIN TO SHIFT FROM "I" TO "WE"

Schooling and the host culture encourage us to exercise our individuality. In the corporate arena, however, the emphasis is on sameness. To succeed, you must blend your personal characteristics with those of the corporate environment to complement and further the goals and objectives of your organization. *No seas yo-yo.*

This is not to say, however, that once you become part of a team, you must forget about or hide your special talents and attributes. Just the opposite.

> **Each member brings his or her own skills, strengths, and vision to enhance the efforts of the team.**

Let's imagine all these wonderful mangos, papayas, guavas, and magueys. Individually, each one is magnificent. You can combine them, however, either one of two ways. You can mush them together and get a delicious marmalade, but you won't be able to distinguish the individual flavors. Or you can make a fruit salad, where each slice of mango, papaya, or guava is easily identifiable by the unique taste it brings to this *ensalada sabrosa.*

Like in the salad, in the corporate arena it is the combination of individual contributions that results in the ultimate success of the team. There is a fine line between "I" and "we." Learn to navigate it.

RULE EIGHT: EVEN IF YOU GET NO DIRECT FEEDBACK, DON'T THINK THEY'RE NOT TALKING ABOUT YOU

In the corporate world, people are always talking *about* you, even if they're not talking *with* you. It is up to you to use your sensitivity and insight to catch the indirect signals being sent your way by upper management.

> **The first tenet of the executive suite is that if you're not smart enough to figure out the rules, you don't belong there. The rules are informal, however, with the assumption being that you will be tuned in enough to understand and follow them.**

The amount of feedback you receive tends to diminish as you progress within an organization. As a result, you must develop the proper skills to interpret your company's culture. Ask yourself such questions as: Is my boss sending me certain signs—a nod, a smile, a specific assignment? Do we have a shared sense of trust? Are our values compatible? How do my coworkers respond to my suggestions, my direction, my style?

> **When you are being supervised, mentored, or coached, insist on being told what you need to hear, not what you'd like to hear.**

As you move within an organization, your vision begins to broaden. Details are typically managed and handled at the lower echelons of the company; the higher in the corporate structure you rise, the more big-picture and visionary you are expected to be.

> **Learn the etiquette of the executive suite and conform to it.**

For example, successful executives are expected to maintain their composure under stress. They handle mistakes with poise and grace. They focus on problems and solve them. They get along with all kinds of people. They might be outspoken, but they're never offensive.

There is no such thing as a crisis at the upper echelons of an organization. There are merely issues that need to be handled. Crisis management, or how we behave in stressful situations, is of critical importance for Latino executives, since we are often stereotyped as being highly emotional. If you act in a manner that leads to your being considered too excitable, the assumption will be that you will fold under pressure. You must always be calm, confident, and predictable.

Recently I was at a high-level business meeting in New York during a terrible snowstorm that paralyzed the whole East Coast. We could see the storm coming in, and by early afternoon it hit with a vengeance. Within an hour, Manhattan was virtually shut down.

An executive who lived in an outlying suburb was concerned that the bridges and tunnels leaving the city would be clogged with traffic or even closed. He became visibly agitated and distressed. He left the meeting to call his family to let them know he would be home late or maybe not at all.

To this day, when that same group of people meet, let one drop of rain fall, and invariably someone says, "Oh, Sam, you'd better call home. You might be late." He has been typecast as a person who believes everything is a crisis, who worries when the weather gets bad. Even though Sam was being considerate of his wife and children, he projected the image of a man who couldn't handle the pressure of sudden emergencies. Do you think he now gets a lot of projects out of that group? Not very likely.

Even though no one will tell you directly, your demeanor and actions are always being judged. For example, the unwritten rules declare that you should never go on the defensive or blame others if you make an error. You should show poise and grace under pressure. The corporate way of handling mistakes is to admit you were wrong, tell other people about your error, and warn them that they should be aware of any possible repercussions. Then analyze and try to repair the problem. This shows integrity and loyalty to the company.

> **Don't wait for someone in the organization to tell you when you have misstepped. Maybe no one will. It is up to you to figure it out and respond accordingly.**

RULE NINE: SHOW RESPECT FOR EVERYONE IN THE ORGANIZATION, EVEN THOSE YOU HAVE TO IMPRESS THE LEAST

The Latino culture teaches us always to be mindful and respectful of all people—those above us and below us. This philosophy will serve you well in the business world, since it will position you as a team player who is concerned with the good of the company.

> **Loyalty to your organization is one of the most important values in corporate America.**

Because Latinos are stereotyped as outsiders who like to stick together, reaching out to everyone in the organization demonstrates a loyalty and allegiance that supersedes our ethnic background. If you limit your friendships in the workplace only to other Hispanics, you will be viewed as exclusionary, un-American, and uncomfortable with other ethnic groups. "You can take them out of the neighborhood, but you can't take the neighborhood out of them," your colleagues might think. "When push comes to shove, they will favor their people. Listen to them talking in Spanish; they must be conspiring about something."

As Latinos, we have been socialized to develop and foster personal relationships. Our great strength lies in the ability to interact with people, to treat others with dignity, and to form solid alliances. These cultural traits will help you on your climb up the corporate ladder, because they satisfy the requirement that business executives have highly developed social skills.

You must learn to capitalize on your strengths, emphasizing those qualities that will advance your career. But you must also be aware of any potential conflicts between your loyalty to your company and your loyalty to your community.

> **Don't give anyone the chance to question your loyalty. Promote the community, but tie it to the bottom line of the organization.**

Dolores is a middle manager at the headquarters of a fast-food giant. She participated and experienced firsthand the struggle for human dignity and call for justice during the 1960s and 1970s. She is now in corporate America but has never lost the principles for which she fought all her life.

"Some people were surprised when I joined a multinational corporation," she says. "It seemed like such an unlikely match. However, I feel loyal to both my company and my community. I have used my position to show the decision makers in my organization why it makes good business sense for them to reach out to the Hispanic community. It is not only the *right* thing to do, it is the *smart* thing to do. I have tied my goals and objectives to those of my company. No one here questions my loyalty. At the same time, by being able to help other Latinos enter the business world, I have created a win-win situation that I am very proud of."

RULE TEN: OBSERVE, OBSERVE, OBSERVE—THEN FOLLOW

Think of corporate life as traveling to a new country, where you have to learn the customs and language in order to get around. The first step in navigating in this unfamiliar environment is to watch what other people are doing. Observe how they act, how they dress, how they talk, what their rhythm is. This is information that is not readily available in guidebooks. You need to be a keen observer and to develop the skill of reading your environment.

If you have had previous exposure—business school, internships, shadowing programs—your job will be easier. If your parents were professionals, you will have already picked up much of this information, and the corporate culture will feel very natural to you.

Be proactive. Take a look at yourself and benchmark against the successful people in the organization. Study their behavior, their mannerisms, their speech, their style. Then model your behavior after theirs.

Prove that you fit in the culture.

Street smarts and intuition are very important. Let's take the concept of "casual Friday," the one day of the week where you are encouraged to come to work in comfortable clothes. You need to be smart enough to identify what "casual" means in your particular organization. I once worked in an organization where casual Friday meant you were allowed to wear a sports jacket and tie instead of a suit. If I had showed up in chinos and a sweater—informal clothes, in my opinion—it would have been apparent to my supervisors that I "didn't get it," that I was not observant enough to note what other people at the company were wearing on the designated dress-down day.

Labels like "he doesn't get it" tend to stick and become defining characterizations. No one would have told me directly, but they would have said to each other, "Juan's the guy who thinks casual Friday is when you show up like you're going to the beach." And that reputation would follow me around in my career.

Fausto, the human resources executive, remembers his first encounter with corporate dress: "Coming from a community-based work environment, it was definitely an awakening for me to enter the corporate world. I had a whole different orientation of what I thought corporate life was about. I didn't have a clue as to what the success factors were!

"My first corporate position was with a Fortune 100 company. It was an extremely conservative company. It was the early 1970s, and I came to work wearing bell bottoms, a blue velour jacket, and with my hair down to my shoulders. I was walking down the hallway and people were turning to look at me. I was thinking that they must be staring at me because I looked so good. What they were doing was laughing at me because I didn't know how to dress. Obviously, I had no idea of appropriate corporate attire.

"Finally, a Latino who had worked there for a while pulled me into his office. He was about ten years older than I, had a masters degree, and was a very committed Hispanic. He said to me, 'Man, if you're going to work here the first thing you have to do is cut your hair, buy yourself a three-piece suit, and get some wing tips. This velour jacket is not cutting it.' I told him that, hey, I thought I must be looking good because everyone kept on checking me out! I thought I was being admired."

Even if your corporation is sending out mixed messages, it is up to you to find out exactly what is rewarded in the organization. For example, if you work at a company where individual achievement is recognized and promoted but collective efforts are also rewarded, you should gear yourself to be a strong team player. At the same time, take the leadership role in the team and demonstrate that you can motivate, inspire, and guide the other team members.

> **Learn from others if you can't figure out the unspoken rules on your own. Ask questions, find someone to coach you, observe your surroundings. Then check your impressions with someone you trust who will give you appropriate and perceptive input.**

By understanding the unwritten codes and customs of corporate America, you will begin to penetrate the invisible barriers that keep Latino executives from entering top management. Take notice of what is expected of you by your supervisors, your colleagues, and the company itself, and adjust your behavior accordingly. To get to the top of the corporate ladder, you must observe, adapt, and emulate the behavior of the people who set the tone and style of your company.

In an information-driven
environment, knowledge
is power.

Knowing the rules of the game
is critical to survival.

If you are going to be a player,
learn to play on their court.

When I first took a job in corporate America, my former mentor, César Chavez, urged me to hold true to my principles. "If they offer you a company car," he advised me, "don't get leather seats."

When I asked César for an explanation, he told me that the more comforts and perks I received, the more I would get used to them and the harder it would be to give them up. "When you fear losing something you have become accustomed to, it makes it more difficult to take those tough stances that may put your perks in jeopardy," he said.

Eventually I was given a company car. But I remembered César's words and chose the one with the fewest amenities. When my boss asked me why I wanted such a plain automobile, I told him that I never wanted to get used to leather seats, because I always wanted to feel free to speak my mind. I did, however, indulge myself with vanity license plates!

—OLGA AROS

STAFF DIRECTOR, DIVERSITY DEVELOPMENT

McDONALD'S CORPORATION

CHAPTER 6

DOES GETTING AHEAD MEAN SELLING OUT?

Grieving Your Success

No hay rosa sin espina.
No pain, no gain.

Victor, the son of immigrants from the Dominican Republic, was the first in his family to get a college degree. Intelligent, ambitious, and determined, he has worked hard to build a successful business career. Victor's efforts have paid off: he has recently been promoted to become director of marketing of the major pharmaceutical company where he has worked for several years, making him the highest-ranking Hispanic in the history of the organization.

Proud of his accomplishments and eager to provide his family with the comforts afforded by his hefty salary increase, Victor decided to sell his small house in the Bronx and purchase a large home in an affluent New Jersey suburb. After settling in, he invited his family and some intimate childhood friends to a housewarming party. Circulating among the guests on his custom-built deck overlooking a huge backyard, Victor is certain that he has finally achieved the American dream.

"So what do you think?" he asks his cousin, a New York City bus driver. "How do you like my place?"

"*Hombre*, you sure moved far from the neighborhood," his cousin answers jokingly. "I had to pack a lunch and show my green card twice to get out here!"

Victor laughs but is suddenly filled with doubts. Is he using his newfound prosperity to leave his roots behind? Is he trying to pass for someone he's not? Does he feel ashamed of being Latino? Is that why he moved to this exclusive area? Victor fights against the urge to apologize to his cousin for exhibiting the trappings of his success. And as Victor continues to think about how far away from where he started out he is, it slowly begins to dawn on him that he is leaving behind a large part of his past as he makes his way up in the corporate world. This is a normal reaction as he learns to combine his two different worlds.

Like Victor, you will face a wide array of challenges and conflicts when your career starts to take off and you find yourself in a social and professional environment different from the one in which you were raised. You must respect both the positive and negative aspects of change and keep in mind the importance of managing change throughout your career.

EMBRACING CHANGE

John F. Kennedy said: "Change is the law of life, and those who look only to the past are certain to miss the future." Yet even as you embrace change you must always be aware of the feelings that accompany it.

Getting ahead causes us to question our motives and priorities: Are we are selling out? Are we turning our backs on our culture? Are we choosing mainstream America over our Latino heritage?

While the phenomenon of questioning success is not exclusive to Latinos, our strong ties to culture and community do create conflict as we move on. You must acknowledge that it exists and learn to deal with it. As Victor came to realize after he moved away from his old neighborhood, all changes, even good ones, are inevitably followed by a sense of loss and a grieving for how things used to be. As you begin your climb up the corporate ladder, you have to prepare yourself for the possibility of feeling alienated and isolated from the very people you expect to be the most supportive.

Most of us think of grieving as something we do when bad things happen to us. But we also grieve when we leave behind the familiar and move into the unfamiliar. Becoming successful means abandoning a certain way of life and leaving some friends and relatives who choose to stay behind.

You must grieve and go on.

"The higher I advance within my organization, the harder it is to spend time with my friends from the old neighborhood," says Tomás, an assistant vice president at a real estate company. "I feel as if I'm living a dual life. When I hang out with the guys I've grown up with, I dress differently, speak differently, even walk differently than I do at work. Sometimes I get confused with my friends and slip into my 'professional' mode. When that happens, I can feel them pulling away from me, and I begin to ask myself if I am selling out, if I am doing the right thing by trying to get ahead. But the default position is to go back to what I know and what I'm comfortable with—the old friends, the old neighborhood, the old surroundings. It creates a lot of conflict.

"My brother drives a delivery truck," Tomás continues. "Soon after I started work at my company, I called my mom and told her there was so much more potential for him. That he could go to college and do more with his life. Her answer was, 'Your brother has a steady job. He's paying his bills.' I dropped it, but I know I have to be very careful. It's very easy to be sucked back into what is familiar and predictable."

We all live with constant change. Yet change is a scary process. Initially you may want to fight it, to negotiate the terms, to cut a deal, even to ignore it and hope it will go away. There are some people who can never accept change. They dwell in the past, remembering how things used to be in the "good old days." These people are uncomfortable with change because they fear it. They are afraid of the effect it will have on their life, how it might disrupt their daily routine, what it will mean for their future.

> **To succeed in the business world, it is not enough to have state-of-the-art information and cutting-edge skills. You must learn to embrace change—not fear it—and welcome the opportunities that new beginnings present.**

MANAGING CHANGE

Beatriz had been with the information systems department of a large insurance company for about a year when she was offered a chance to move up. The company was preparing to phase in new software and was looking for people to train the staff. Beatriz's supervisors, impressed with her sharp intelligence and willingness to pitch in, recommended her for the training program. She would have to complete a three-month course to learn the program and would then become an information systems training manager.

Beatriz was flattered to be given the opportunity to advance but was terrified that she might fail to live up to her bosses' expectations. "What if I can't learn this new complicated software system?" she asked herself. "What happens if I find myself in over my head?"

Beatriz knew she could do her job very well and that she would be safe if she stayed where she was. Yet she also knew that if she turned down management's offer, she would never be given another chance to move ahead in her company. Beatriz took a deep breath, enrolled in the course, and ended up being the star pupil in her class. She now heads the in-house training program in her organization and is in line for yet another promotion.

> **It is perfectly normal to be afraid of change. But don't allow your fears to stand in the way of accepting the challenges that will be continually presented to you on your way up the corporate ladder.**

The changes we confront in our careers are not just technological. Managerial styles are also constantly being invented and reinvented. For example, your organization may presently reward individual accomplishments and star performance. Then one day management hires a productivity consultant, and teamwork becomes the preferred mode of operating. Or your corporation decides to reorganize, downsize, or rightsize and eliminates entire departments and divisions or creates new ones. Don't be the person who says, "It was better the old way." You must be flexible and willing to try new forms of management.

If you are reluctant to change, you will be labeled a resister. Most change efforts have to do with redistribution of power and learning. In order to manage change, you must be willing to unlearn old behaviors and learn the new behaviors. The issue of redistribution of power has a social and political dimension to it. If you align with and support those persons effecting change, they will help you ascend the corporate ladder.

> **Change can move a career, jump-start a career, regenerate a career, or stifle a career—it's your choice.**

The changes that come with succeeding in your career are bound to spill over to your personal life. As you move up in management you will have new social obligations that you will need to meet. You might be encouraged to join certain organizations, attend charity functions, or participate in some nonprofit work.

This is part of participating in the all-important informal business networks. You must do these things to build relationships with people who can help you with your career.

Eventually you will have to make choices and set priorities. You may find you no longer have the time to go and shoot hoops with your buddies on a Thursday evening or to take a long drive on Saturday morning to the old neighborhood to get the *pan* and *frutas* that are not available where you now live. These changes can be very painful because they may make you feel as if you are relinquishing a part of your past. The reality is that you are.

As you move ahead in your career, it will not only be your friends outside the office whom you will be leaving behind. Let's say you are promoted into an executive position. You will now spend most of your time with others in management. When you go to lunch at the company cafeteria, you may want to sit with your former coworkers, but when you enter the room someone from your new peer group is likely to call over to you: "I'm glad you're here. Come join us. We have a lot to talk about."

It may be conscious or unconscious, but you will find yourself gravitating toward people on the same level as yourself. And you may hear comments such as, "Look at him. Mister Big Shot. He used to hang out with us, but now he's too good to sit at our table."

> **It is normal to grieve what you have left behind. It is a real loss. Change causes turmoil, and you will feel torn for a time, pulled in two directions.**

You will also encounter a tremendous amount of pressure from your new peer group as you rise within your organization's hierarchy. As management accepts you as one of them they begin to expect you to live up to the standards of their community. You have to represent what they stand for and adapt your behavior accordingly.

"I think that some people don't dare to take that step forward because they're afraid to appear to be deserting their roots, abandoning the cause," says Mario, an investment banker. "But if you're too concerned about the cause, it will consume you. You must walk forward without worrying that you are taking something with you or leaving other things behind. Then you're going to be fine.

"We are told that we need to look out for our community first and then approach the outside. I was taught, and I was allowed to learn, to trust in myself and go out there to represent my people. But you don't have to bring that flag with you. You don't have to carry the sign with you. Just go out as an individual. What you have—what you are—is inside of you. Meet the people in corporate America. Show them you respect them. Gain their respect in return. And then come back and share your journey with your people. That's what I did, and it helps me with reconciling my two worlds."

> As you move up the corporate ladder, you must blend your professional identity with a new set of social and civic obligations. You will have to leave behind certain parts of your old life, because they will not fit with your new image. This loss of a part of yourself will be very sad. Deal with these feelings; don't ignore them. Allow the grieving process to run its cycle, otherwise you will get stuck and stagnate. You will emerge stronger at the end.

SOCIAL CHANGE

Pete, a sales manager at a large company, decided to have a party at his house. He invited some of his colleagues and several of his friends and neighbors from *el barrio*. It was the first time Pete, the son of Colombian immigrants, was mixing his professional and personal worlds, and he was anxious about how everyone would get along. He thought the party should be more "American" than "Hispano." Instead of serving *sancocho* and *arepas*, he had the food catered by a local upscale restaurant. And rather than play his *cumbia* music, he put on some low-key jazz.

Even though there was very little mingling between his friends and his colleagues, Pete considered the party a success. When he went to work on Monday, his impression was reinforced by the enthusiastic response of the people in the office who attended the party. "It was so much fun," they said. "We really enjoyed ourselves."

Pete's Latino friends, on the other hand, couldn't figure out what was going on. "Pete used to be the life of the party," they said to each other afterward, "always making jokes, dancing up a storm. But now there was no dancing, just stuffy conversation—and all in English. The food looked beautiful, but the portions were so small that you left the party hungry. ¡Qué vergüenza! Has Pete become a social climber? What's happened to this guy? Has he turned his back on his Latino background just to be acceptable to the people at work?"

Pete probably did not make jokes in Spanish because he didn't want his non-Latino guests to feel left out. Perhaps he decided against serving spicy food and playing Colombian music because he thought it wouldn't fit in with the mood of the evening. Or possibly his friends' observations are true: Maybe Pete was subconsciously trying so hard to assimilate into the white culture of his work environment that he was attempting to erase any reminders of his Hispanic upbringing.

Like Pete, you will constantly face the conflicts of acculturation and assimilation as you move up the corporate ladder and conform to the customs and traits of corporate America's host culture. Many Latino executives choose to deal with these conflicts by keeping their professional and personal lives very separate from each other. Others find ways to blend work and heritage.

Once you achieve a degree of professional success and attain a certain status, you will probably feel more secure.

> **On your way up, however, you must be very aware of being perceived as appearing too ethnic and different from the rest of the people in your organization. This will not provide the comfort and fit necessary for promotion.**

You will feel sad about giving up—or putting on hold—those parts of your culture that are familiar and dear to you. But remember, the grieving is not just about loss, it is also a reaction to change. There will always be some ambivalence, like Victor's mixed feelings about his new house. There will always be a part of you that misses your old apartment, your familiar neighborhood, your childhood friends. The sad irony is that you will not be able to discuss these feelings with some of your closest *familia* and *cuates*. "What are you complaining about?" they will probably respond, unable to put themselves in your place. "You have money and status. What else do you need?"

> **No one will feel sorry for you because of your success. As a result, you may feel alienated and isolated, keeping your pain and confusion to yourself. For a time you may be very, very lonely.**

MOVING AHEAD, LEAVING BEHIND

When you leave your former lifestyle and peers behind, some will react to your success with envy. How is it possible that you made it as far as you did? What did you have to do to get ahead? Do you now think you are better than everyone else?

"I'm the first person in my entire extended family to graduate from college," says Rafael, an executive in an oil company. "I don't think that I've lost my Cuban identity because I've succeeded in the corporate world. I have a lot of pride in my roots, and I still enjoy my *café con leche* and listening to salsa. Yet when I visit my cousins in Miami and they see me walking out of the airport with my blond wife and golf clubs, they automatically assume I've become an Anglo. Our community sometimes has an aversion to mixing. But I'm not afraid of losing myself. My folks taught me that I should always first see myself as an individual, so I am proud of having built a life that allows me to enjoy a blend of cultures. To be honest, though, sometimes I feel defensive about my choices and wonder if I've given up more of my Latino roots than I think."

Most of us don't think of success as something that produces problems and conflicts. "This should be easy," you tell yourself. "I have worked hard. I deserve the professional recognition and financial security. I should be happy."

> **But as you move ahead, you will discard some important parts of your upbringing, and you will miss them. These feelings should not stop you from continuing the climb, but you must acknowledge and honor them.**

Hispanic culture recognizes professional achievement in terms not only of economics but also of contribution to the community. Leaders of nonprofit organizations and educators, for example, are afforded positions of respect because of the importance and significance of their work. Business executives, on the other hand, are often perceived to be the bad guys. There is a widespread notion among Latinos that corporate America is not being responsive to the needs of our people.

It is up to you to begin to change this view and to bridge the gap between the Latino and corporate communities. For example, I was recently on a panel dealing with the issue of how best to educate Hispanic youths. The consensus was that the national public school system was in crisis and that it was crucial for corporations to offer financial and technical assistance. The experts on the panels agreed that more Latino children than ever before are dropping out of school or are graduating without basic reading and writing skills.

My job as a corporate insider was to coach the people in the audience on how to present their message in terms that the business world could understand. I had to explain how to speak the language of corporations, how to communicate the most effective approach to use when asking for funds from the mostly white business executives who control the purse strings of their companies.

I pointed out that corporations are hearing a dual message. On the one hand, they are told that the system is failing Latino children, that the schools are not well equipped, that the dropout rate is high, that gangs are running wild in the schools, and so on. On the other hand, they are told that more Latinos than ever are graduating from college and getting MBAs and that we should be given more opportunities to advance into upper management.

What is the corporate response? "Wait a minute," they tell the Latino community. "You're saying you're smarter than ever before, but at the same time you're saying your children are underskilled and undereducated. So which is it?" This dual message causes the corporate world to question the integrity of the group or organization asking for support.

As more and more Hispanics join the ranks of corporate America, it is our responsibility to share our success and to coach other Latinos. That way you can turn grieving your success into helping our people. Let them know how the game is played, how to solicit funds, how to get hired, how to gain corporate sponsorship.

> **Share your inside information with other members of the Latino community.**

Throughout this process, you have to remember that your first loyalty is to your organization. You might hear comments like, "We're asking you to help us because you're Hispanic. You owe that to us. Your commitment to your community should be more important than your allegiance to your company." Your response should be: "Do you want me to help other Hispanics merely because they're Latino or because they're the best person for the position?" Or "My company would like to fund the most worthy organization, based on merit. Help me show that your group fits the bill."

Part of your responsibility as a trailblazer is to afford opportunities—not handouts—to others. The African American community uses a great term for this: *Hand up, not handout.* For many years, our people have been excluded from the competition. As a successful Latino, you need to encourage other Hispanics to prepare for the race, to share with them the secrets of training for and gaining access to the competition. With your help, the success and achievements of our people in the business world will be based on skills and intelligence, not quotas and special privileges.

LETTING GO OF THE LOSS

It doesn't matter where you come from—there is always a sense of loss that accompanies success. Many people who achieve professional recognition feel isolated from everybody else. It is important to acknowledge these feelings and to be prepared for their impact on your personal life and career.

"When I told my parents I had been accepted to Columbia University Business School, my father was quite upset," says Rosario, the bank vice president. "Even though I was going to an Ivy League school, my dad seemed more concerned about my appearing modest about what I had achieved. He didn't want me going around acting as if I were smarter than everyone else.

"In undergraduate school, I paid my whole way. I worked at all these different jobs, because I didn't even realize that I could get financial aid. My parents couldn't guide me on this. So I thought I would have to pay for myself, and I did. I paid my tuition, for all my books and everything else. By the time I entered business school, I didn't have any undergraduate debt.

"But these kinds of things happen when you're the child of an immigrant and don't have a whole lot of places to go for help. My family had always been timid about asking for guidance. My dad had this thing that you don't ask other people for help. You should be independent and figure it out yourself.

"I don't see how I could have really changed things, given my upbringing. But I wish I had more self-confidence when I started out. I received a full scholarship at Columbia, but I was very nervous for the first few weeks of class because I thought they made a mistake. I was sure that any second I would be told that someone had goofed up, and I hadn't received a scholarship at all.

"Finally I went to the admissions office and asked why they had given me the scholarship. They thought this was really amusing. Then the admissions director told me that one of the things that really stood out in my application was that I used to compete in rodeos when I was young! Later on, I read someplace that if you do anything unusual or interesting, you should make sure to write it on your application because it will be memorable. And to me, being in the rodeo was part of my upbringing. It might feel very far away from my life now, but it was very much part of me then.

"When my mom and dad went to my graduation, the whole flight from Texas to New York, my mom kept saying, 'I can't believe this. What is Rosario doing so far away?' But once they got here and met my fellow students, they were really impressed with what I had accomplished. When they saw me receive my degree, it suddenly hit them how far I had come. Their entire opinion of the choices I had made with my life changed. They told me how proud they were of me.

"I am the only one of my brothers and sisters to go to college, let alone receive an MBA. But I have ten nieces and nephews, all under the age of eleven. And each of my brothers and sisters—and my parents, too—are very, very committed to making sure they go on to college, because of my experience. So it's been worth it, definitely worth it. But it's been a very big struggle, that's the truth."

The reality is that most of us are very scared of change. We stay in relationships; we stay in our hometowns; we stay in jobs; we stay in all kinds of situations because we are frightened of the unknown.

To embrace change, you have to look at it as a positive experience. Personally, I like change. I like the adventure, the learning, the anticipation, the desire to know what's around the next corner. It's exciting and challenging. And the bottom line is that there is no other choice.

You cannot advance in the corporate arena without accepting change.

Organizations and people who don't embrace change end up like the dinosaurs—everything passes them by. You must always keep moving. We are all agents of change, but you have to decide which type of change fits you best, evolution or revolution.

You don't have to take quantum leaps in order to change, however. Take one step, then refine; take another step, then refine again. Some organizations, for example, are continuously redefining themselves by constantly reviewing their current situation. It's an ongoing life cycle: They spin off a new venture, evaluate it, then test a new version of it. They are always doing something new and moving ahead. You can follow the same pattern in your career.

> **Develop a strategy for change. Incorporate as many people as possible into the process by sharing your plans as soon as you have clearly formulated them. If you see yourself as a work in process, then you are always seeking to better yourself. You will soon realize that the current version is the best version out for now, until you improve it.**

Letting go of the pain and sense of loss means coming to terms with the guilt of succeeding and leaving many parts of your old identity behind. This can be very difficult. Sometimes I swear that our mothers all got together and decided to really go heavy on the guilt in raising their sons and daughters. That's part of the problem. We do something great—like succeeding in our career—and before we can celebrate our accomplishments, we have to go through the obligatory guilt trip.

I remember when I first began to allow myself to feel happy and proud of my professional and financial success. I had been sent by my company to work on a project in Mexico City. I was excited to return as an up-and-coming executive to the city where I had lived many years before as a graduate student.

Then, I had lived in my uncle's apartment building in a lower-middle-class neighborhood. The apartment lacked some of the creature comforts one becomes accustomed to in the United States. The floors were concrete, the rooms were cold, and the water was erratic, especially in the summer. The hot water heater had to be ignited every time you wanted to shower, and there was no shower stall, just a shower head that stuck out of the wall and sprayed the whole bathroom. The electricity was often interrupted without warning.

Either I didn't notice it then, or none of this mattered to me as a young graduate student. But I remembered living in that apartment and picturing myself staying in one of those fancy downtown hotels, cutting deals during the day and relaxing at night. And here I was on my triumphant return, heading for one of Mexico's finest hotels, in the heart of the city's posh Chapultepec area.

Of course I stopped by to see my uncle—what good is a triumphant return if no one sees you? Then I got hit with a dose of Mom's guilt. "Your *padres* told me you were coming here on business," he said, giving me a huge *abrazo*. "I had the porter prepare an apartment for you. Surely you'll stay here."

"Oh, my God," I thought. "Good-bye marble lobby, good-bye swimming pool, good-bye king-size bed, good-bye hot water, good-bye *mariachis* in the bar. Hello cold floors." I had to make a quick decision. I thanked my uncle and told him that my company had booked a room for me in a hotel. "Why don't you accompany me there so I can cancel the reservation?" I asked.

When we arrived at the hotel, my uncle reminded me that I had always pointed out these types of places to him when I was a student, promising that one day I would be staying there as a guest. Then he said, "Why don't you keep the room anyway, in case some of your meetings ever run late? That way you don't have to drive all the way home late at night. Or maybe you'll need a place to freshen up or rest during the day."

So I checked in. We went to see the room. My uncle's eyes lit up when he saw the luxurious surroundings. Then he beamed with pride. "Stay here," he told me. "Be close to your work and your colleagues. I'll come visit you here. *Hijo*, I'm glad you went to school. I'm glad you were a good student and got an education. I'm glad your dreams came true. You deserve all your success."

Gracias, Tío.

**A sense of loss
accompanies success.**

**It's natural to grieve change,
even good change.**

**Letting go doesn't mean
you don't care.**

Pay careful attention to the management of your career. In the corporate world there are essentially three career categories:

- The top 1 percent. These are the stars, those individuals who are highly sought after. Their careers are carefully mapped, guided, and protected.
- The bottom 5 percent. These careers have hit troubled waters from their inception. They never get going, so consequently there is no career to manage.
- The majority fall somewhere in between and in some regards are at the greatest risk of career mismanagement. These individuals are generally strong, solid performers with good credentials. They do consistent, dependable work. As a result, they tend to receive positive feedback. Too often these individuals fall into a trap. They are lulled into thinking that someone is looking out for them, taking notice, and that they will be rewarded for their hard work and devoted service to the organization. What they get is a cycle of more work and more pats on the back. They have become utility players—backroom, behind-the-scenes worker bees, with carrots always dangling just slightly out of reach.

Too many of our people are in this category. Too many figure it out too late, when they are comfortable enough to not risk making waves or starting all over again. Don't wait to be taken care of—take care of yourself.

To avoid this trap, be proactive in your career. Focus on the job that needs to be done and don't get stuck on the position. It is advisable to identify a successful individual or individuals in your company or industry whose career you would most like to emulate. Get to know them. Find out what strengths they have. Learn how they overcame weaknesses. Focus on their skills and experiences. Try to acquire the ones that would be most helpful to you.

Tactfully publicize your good results, even (especially) if doing so doesn't come naturally to you. Always stay open to opportunities, within and outside of your company. Avoid behaviors that are completely foreign to your company's culture.

—LUIS NIETO
EXECUTIVE VICE PRESIDENT OF MARKETING,
SALES, AND DISTRIBUTION
MISSION FOODS

CHAPTER 7

LIGHTING CANDLES TO THE VIRGIN AND OTHER PROVEN CAREER ADVANCEMENT STRATEGIES

El que no arriesga, no gana.
Nothing ventured, nothing gained.

"Mamá, I am being considered for a position that just opened up in my department. It would be a promotion for me."

"*Si Dios quiere*, God willing. *Hijo,* if this is what you really want, tomorrow in church I will light a candle to the Virgin."

Our mothers' prayers are always welcome. But those of us who want to succeed in the business arena must take care of the terrestrial forces that shape our careers by carefully developing a strategy for climbing the corporate ladder. You have to design a step-by-step plan to enhance your performance, image, and profile within your company in order to position yourself to be noticed by the decision makers. *Apodérate*—it's all about empowerment.

Los viejos teach us that hard work and diligence guarantee success.

> **Even though perseverance and dedication are important ingre-
> dients in the formula for getting ahead, it is your profile and
> visibility within your company that lead to eventual promotion.**

What good is it to be a top performer if no one notices you or someone else gets the credit for your work? To advance, you have to be good at your job and at letting people in power know what a good job you are doing.

The management of your performance, image, and profile cannot be left to chance. Decision makers don't just "happen" to notice someone's good work. They keep an eye on those individuals whom they have identified as potential leaders. They assign these men and women to key, high-profile projects, allowing them to be creative and promoting their ideas with upper management.

In order to advance your career you must:

- Position yourself within the organization.
- Network and get assigned to attention-getting projects that will attract notice.
- Know when to cut your losses.
- Respect the *política* of when and how to call in favors.
- Overcome your *vergüenza* about asking for help.
- Make certain to choose your battles carefully.
- Adjust the precepts of your Hispanic background to reflect the identity of the organization where you work.
- Formulate a personal strategy for being mentored and sponsored into the upper echelons of organizational management.

> **Remember, PIP: Performance, Image, and Profile. And a good
> word from your mother and a candle to the Virgin here and
> there certainly won't hurt!**

PERFORMANCE—HARD WORK ALONE ISN'T ENOUGH

It is a given that you must produce high-quality work that is both timely and informed. Your efforts should make your supervisors take notice of the talent and commitment you bring to your job. But hard work in and of itself is not enough to make you stand out among your coworkers. Your individual strategy for gaining entry into the upper echelons of management must incorporate a marketing plan for your most important product—yourself.

If you expect responsibility and power to be automatically conferred on you because you are a top performer, you're in for a very long wait. There are few people whose careers progress on the strength of performance alone. You have to work with the understanding that no one cares about your professional ambitions as much as you do and that it is therefore *your* responsibility to do everything possible to promote your own career.

> Be proactive in planning your career advancement strategy. Devise a game plan that will position you on the executive track. Market yourself in a way that will ensure that you get assigned visible and significant projects. Let decision makers know about your accomplishments.

To begin, do not get pigeonholed within the organization. According to the Hispanic Policy Development Project of the Mauricio Gaston Institute, the majority of Hispanics in the private sector end up in staff positions that offer little career mobility and limited access to leadership development programs and mentoring. Latinos are usually clustered in such areas as community relations, human resources, public affairs, and corporate giving, departments that historically provide minimal opportunities for advancement into upper management.

Look at the senior executives in your organization and see where they started in their careers. If most top managers came from marketing, finance, or sales, then position yourself to enter one of these bottom-line departments. Your objective is to get your foot in the door, so take advantage of whatever opportunity presents itself in the area where you would like to work. Even if your job does not initially give you the kind of exposure you will eventually need, working in one of your company's key departments will help you accumulate inside knowledge of your company's business and get to know people who might be important to you later on in your career.

Let's consider Susana as an example. She's been a human resources representative with her company for three years. During this time, both her responsibilities and her salary have steadily increased. Susana is proud of her excellent record, but she is beginning to get nervous that her career will dead-end in human resources. "Am I bumping my head against the glass ceiling that people talk about?" she asks herself.

Susana decides to formulate a plan to move her career along. She knows that she needs to increase her visibility within the company. She does some research and finds out that the action in her organization is happening over in marketing. Management considers it a key to profitability and closely monitors the department's performance. The marketing staff, therefore, receives a lot of attention and recognition.

There are no openings in the marketing department for the moment, though. Rather than throw her hands up in defeat, Susana does some more asking around to see what other departments are "hot." She learns that several of the company's vice presidents started out in finance. And as luck would have it, Susana knows that a position in finance will become available in a couple of months.

Now Susana faces a different challenge. Although she took some finance and accounting courses in college, her skills in this area are a little rough. To give herself a better shot at getting the job, Susana enrolls in an accounting course in a community college and attends classes three nights a week. She also lets the finance manager know that she is interested in working in that department. When the position in finance finally opens up, the manager is impressed by Susana's initiative and motivation. "This one has the fire in the belly to get ahead," her future boss concludes, and Susana beats out more than thirty other applicants for the job.

Like Susana, you should formulate a strategy to further your professional goals. Your plan should include a time frame and a realistic assessment of opportunities for advancement within your organization.

Make Your Intentions Known

Be vocal about your desire to advance. Tell your supervisors that you are willing to accept additional responsibilities and assignments. Demonstrate that you have initiative and are inventive. Search out opportunities that will allow you to grow beyond the scope of your current work. Keep in mind the delicate balance between appearing ambitious and seeming pushy. You must be careful not to be disrespectful to other people on your way up the corporate ladder—you never know when you'll meet them again.

Show Flexibility and Interest

Although you must stay focused on your present position, make it clear that you are enthusiastic about venturing into new areas or projects. Managers will not come to you with offers to work for them unless they know of your interest and intentions to advance. Don't allow inertia to stop you from making a move.

Be open and flexible when you consider opportunities for advancement. Don't hold out for that dream job, because you never know what route may take you there.

Keep Improving Your Qualifications

No matter how good you are at your job, there is always room to grow. Take courses, attend seminars, go to conferences. Don't limit yourself to your immediate area. Prepare to be a corporate leader by developing and honing your skills in as many aspects of management as you can. Don't neglect your facility with the Spanish language. Remember, *quien habla dos lenguas vale por dos*. One who is bilingual is worth two people.

Don't Just Perform, Outperform

If you have a reputation for doing good work, being dependable, and delivering on time, you will get better assignments. Even if you lack some of the skills necessary for the project, you'll be invited to join the team if your supervisors know they can count on you.

You must demonstrate your passion for hard work, based on your own professional pride and your loyalty to the organization. Keep in mind that regardless of what your area of expertise is or the type of organization you work for, marketing and sales are a part of everything you do.

You must constantly promote yourself and your ideas.

For example, if your company is losing money but you're in a department that's profitable, you have to show management how you have helped buck the downward trend for the organization. Conversely, if your company is flush but you have the bad luck to be in a nonperforming unit, make sure your positive contributions to the profitability of the corporation are well documented for future reference.

If you have an idea or have completed an assignment success-fully, overcome the cultural inhibitions of your Latino upbringing that discourage you from promoting yourself, out of fear of appearing too pushy or forward. Let people know about your projects and accomplishments: Prepare a memo for your division head outlining your new marketing plan; talk up the increase in your unit's profits to people in other departments; share your enthusiasm with your coworkers.

> **Being shy and retiring is a sure career killer. If you wait to be asked instead of volunteering, management will assume you're just not interested.**

Benchmark Your Progress Against Others in Your Company

You can always compare your progress to that of your coworkers and other people who started with your company at approximately the same time you did. Better yet, look at the career paths of the successful men and women in your organization to see what route they took to rise in the ranks of management.

You always want to benchmark with those who are higher up than you.

> **You benchmark with success.**

If others have started with you and you have surpassed them, don't worry about them anymore. If you measure against people below you, you might get complacent and feel you are doing better than you actually are. *En el mundo de los ciegos el tuerto es rey.* In the land of the blind, the one-eyed man is king.

"I was hired for an internship program right out of business school," explains Pablo, a Cuban American stockbroker from Chicago. "I soon noticed that the people I started out with who were white were getting better projects and moving ahead faster than I was. I think it was because the bosses felt more comfortable with them than with those of us who were black or Hispanic. I began to understand that in business, who you know determines whether you get ahead and how fast. You have to have the right connections to begin with or make them along the way.

"I decided it was up to me to make the effort if I wanted to get noticed. I would have to pick up the phone or make an appointment to see someone and say, 'Hey, I'm interested in this position on your team,' or 'I'd really like to participate in your project.' I couldn't wait for opportunities to come to me—I would have to seek them out.

"I was very hesitant at first. The Hispanic culture teaches us not to be aggressive, so calling attention to myself went against everything I learned growing up. But it was the only way I had to keep up with the progress of others at my level.

"I believe there is a tremendous amount of opportunity for success for our people. In a few years, I bet more than half the population of the United States will speak Spanish. I'm looking forward to that day, because I'm going to be saying, 'Sure, I speak Spanish. And of course I'd be willing to consider your job offer!' "

IMAGE—THE LOOK IS MORE THAN SKIN-DEEP

Even if you are performing at your highest capacity and are well respected in the company for your technical skills and quick intellect, you will not move ahead if you are perceived as lacking an executive presence.

> You must look the part and communicate an aura of success in order to be promoted into upper management. You have to "walk the talk."

The great majority of messages you send to other people are nonverbal. Even when you are involved in a brief exchange, a myriad of details are communicated, and perceptions are formed. Most people form impressions during the first few minutes of an interaction. People rely on shortcuts to size each other up, and as I mentioned in chapter 3, a very common mental shortcut is stereotyping.

"My first job was as an assistant to an executive vice president of a brokerage firm. I was the only Latino at the company, except for one of the messengers," says Silvia. "Even though my boss was very supportive, one of her colleagues had a very difficult time accepting me. She would call over to me in front of everyone in the office, '*Arriba, arriba*. Let's keep working, Ms. Speedy Gonzalez.'

"I tried not to be too sensitive about her kidding, although to tell you the truth, I didn't find it funny. People like to associate you with the stereotypes of Latinos they see in the media. Maybe it's not meant to be hurtful, but some people haven't been exposed to educated Hispanics, or any Hispanics for that matter. Eventually this woman came to know me and respect me as a person—apart from my being Hispanic. But it was very difficult for me at the beginning."

Because stereotyping allows us to assign positive or negative values in a short time, we end up placing other people into slots based on quick, superficial impressions. Our judgment is influenced by such factors as dress, handshake, posture, eye contact, language, use of space, and so on. Most of us first focus on what we see, then what we hear, then the content of what we are hearing.

You don't get a second chance to make a first impression.

Your appearance, which is constantly judged and evaluated, conveys an extremely important nonverbal message to others in the workplace. Regardless of the dress code in your particular company, you must look as if you are in charge, and carry yourself with a demeanor that communicates authority. Your choice of clothing communicates how you feel about yourself, your level of self-esteem, and your attitude about conforming to your company's standards.

> **Your clothing should be viewed as an investment in your career. Your accessories are the necessary props that should be modeled after those displayed by the top executives in your company. Remember, what you wear sends a message. Dress for the position you want, not the one you have, and at the level of those people whom you want to influence.**

Body language is another key set of nonverbal signals we send to other people. For example, good posture conveys self-assurance and control of the situation. Your mother was right when she told you to sit up straight! This communicates determination and conviction, a sense of assertiveness and success. A firm, brief handshake, accompanied by direct eye contact, shows you are confident and direct.

How we occupy space is also important for conveying a confident image. Extending your physical space extends your influence. Most Latinos are brought up to be modest, to stand in a room quietly without calling attention to themselves. But in the business world, fading into the background or shrinking into a corner sends a message that you are uncomfortable and ill at ease.

> **You must learn to command the space you occupy, because it is an extension of your influence.**

How you maintain your work area is another part of your image. If your office is neat and tidy, your desk clean and orderly, you will give the impression of efficiency. A messy office says that you are not entirely in control of your workload or have an organizational system that is strictly personal and not accessible to anyone else.

The manner in which you decorate your office also projects a very specific image of who you are. Your knickknacks, wall hangings, photographs, desk accessories, and so on should not make anyone who enters your space feel uncomfortable in any way. None of your items should be too personal, ethnic, political, or obscure. Your office should never look too cozy or permanently inhabited, because that will give the impression that you are so comfortable there you may not want to leave.

> **Your objective is to create a professional and personal image that shapes and influences how others view you—as someone on the way up.**

It is part of your job to present yourself in a way that exudes confidence, capability, determination, assertiveness, comfort, and ease. Creating a specific impression is a deliberate process that may sometimes feel like playacting. But it is an important way of getting people to take notice of you, making them comfortable in your presence, and allowing them to see your flexibility and willingness to fit into the corporate culture.

PROFILE—GETTING THE WORD OUT

When you sit down to formulate a plan to increase your visibility within your company, ask yourself the following questions:

- What kind of profile do I have in my organization?
- What kind of projects am I involved in?
- How can I directly impact the bottom line?

The most critical task in your advancement strategy is to communicate to the decision makers in your organization that you possess the qualifications to be a good leader; that you are ready, willing, and able to manage other people; that you are loyal and dependable; and that you can be trusted to perform at your best, at all times, for the good of the organization.

The Winslow Research Institute lists the following characteristics as the core traits of a leader:

- Self-confidence
- Mental toughness
- Conceptual thinking
- Ambition to achieve

In addition, a leader should have a diverse track record, inspire trust and confidence, maintain composure under stress, handle mistakes with poise and grace, focus on problems and solve them, be open to risk, be willing to act decisively, motivate and direct others, and be able to get along with all kinds of people.

How can you achieve the necessary access to show your worth as a leader? The first step is to prove to the decision makers in your company that you have the *comfort* and *fit* required for sponsorship into senior management. Next you must promote your accomplishments and make them known to your boss and your boss's boss.

Get connected! Begin to network on a variety of levels—with your peers, your supervisors, your colleagues in other companies. Networking activities can be formal or informal, professional or social, civic or recreational. Use these occasions to tell others about your accomplishments and your goals. Always keep your eyes and ears open for information about developments and opportunities in your field.

Saber es tener poder. Those who have the knowledge have the power.

> **Information management is information control.**

In management, deciding who gets to know what can be used as a way to promote or exclude individuals. Make sure you stay in the loop by nurturing and maintaining connections with people at all levels of your organization.

Remember, as Latinos, we must always contend with stereotypes and work against them. If your demeanor is not polished and convincing, it will reinforce the belief that Hispanics are only being hired by corporate America as a result of quotas and entitlement programs. If you don't project a visual impression that conforms to the organization's image, you will be categorized as an outsider and denied the chance to share your ideas and suggestions with those people who can sponsor you into positions of responsibility and influence. If you hold back from promoting your achievements, you will be perceived as too timid to compete and win.

"I didn't know what office politics were when I started out," says Sara, an executive at a cosmetics company. "Where I come from, everyone was vocal and up front about how they felt and what they wanted. In the corporate world, some people will say one thing but mean something very different. One day you're on their good side, and the next day they avoid you. Things are more covert here.

"It took a lot of getting used to. I knew I had to become visible and aggressive about letting people know who I was and what I wanted. In a corporate environment, you have to speak up. You can't wait for people to help you along. You must step forward and say, 'I want to do this. I am good at that. I want to get ahead.' "

> **To make yourself known and your presence recognized, you must constantly network. Get connected with as many different people who can help you advance your career as possible. Develop and maintain relationships with those men and women throughout your entire career.**

YOU CAN'T DO IT WITHOUT A MENTOR

The key to success in advancing your career is finding a person who believes in you and will sponsor you into upper management. Mentors, role models, guardian angels, *padrinos*—call them what you like.

> **If you don't have a mentor to show you the way, you will not have a chance to succeed in corporate America.**

"My mentor made sure that I would rise within my company," says Eddie, a marketing representative for a large hospitality organization. "You know what he did? He put his arm around me and said, 'I don't know you. You come from a place I've never been. You have a long last name I can't pronounce. But I've kept my eye on you, I believe in you, and I want to help you.'

"Even though his most recent promotion took him to another city, he still looks after my interests. He calls me all the time. He phones my boss to see how I'm doing. He drops my name at executive staff meetings. Now he's trying to find an opening for me in his current office.

"One of the reasons I work so hard is that I don't want to let my mentor down or disappoint him. He is an established and respected businessman, and he took a risk with me. I want to show him that he was right in putting his faith in me."

Some companies automatically assign mentors to newly hired staff. Be careful, for there is nothing worse than a bad mentor. No matter what the official company policy is, it is up to you to find your own mentor within the company.

Choose a person you would like to resemble in a few years, instead of trying to find someone who is similar to you now. Develop a strategy for meeting this individual. Look for someone to introduce you, or just approach the person on your own. Make an appointment; engage in conversation at a meeting or after a presentation; demonstrate your knowledge of the person's career and professional background; say you would like to learn more about the company over breakfast, lunch, dinner, coffee, whatever—depending on his or her schedule.

There is a chance that you might be turned down. Don't be discouraged—turn around and choose someone else to ask for help and advice. Never stop looking for that special click that means you've connected with another person.

"It is essential to have a mentor," advises Daniel, the California communications executive. "In the corporate world, you will find that the most successful people have had mentors. That's why they move up the corporate ladder so fast. Not because they're extraordinarily gifted or special. No, it is because a person who cared about their careers opened doors for them, gave them assignments, coached them about the right thing to do, and gave them advice about what was considered acceptable and unacceptable in the company."

How do companies choose among competing candidates for managerial positions? Some organizations consider all the applicants, review their qualifications, experience, and references, and then decide who is best suited for the job. This process is based on *merit* and *objectivity*, placing emphasis on a person's track record and potential.

Most hiring, however, is much more *subjective*. What matters are family connections, school affiliations, membership in clubs, social prejudices, and so on. You must learn to deal with this reality in the corporate arena and try to work around it by creating your own network of potential sponsors and mentors.

"Last year, my division manager asked me to consider hiring a young man right out of college for a fairly responsible position in my department," says Viviana, an investment banker in Los Angeles. "He gave me the young man's résumé, told me that someone in the firm knew the applicant's parents, that he had gone to good schools, and so on. When I looked at the résumé, I just about died. This person's entire experience consisted of working at the pro shop in some tennis club. I remember thinking: 'You have to be kidding. He did go to good schools, but surely you have to have a lot more than that to qualify for investment banking.'

"I went back to the division head and said, 'This gentleman's experience won't even get him one foot in the door.' He answered, 'You know, if he's been working in a tennis club, he probably met one of the firm's partners over there, who likes him and wants to give him a break. But you're right, it seems like a stretch at this point.'

"Well, guess what? A couple of weeks later I found out that the kid was hired by another division of the company. And I was just shocked, really shocked. I had worked my way through college and business school, and it took me five years to get where I am now. And here is someone straight out of school, who's got nothing to show except knowing the right people, and it's not a problem. I understood, then and there, the real power of connections in the business world.

"In retrospect, I'm happy about the path I've taken, because it makes me appreciate everything very much. But am I—and other Latinos, African Americans, women—at a disadvantage? Yes, unless we also find mentors, *on our own*, to help us with our climb up the corporate ladder. I've been very lucky, because one of the women I initially worked with became my guardian angel. She saw my merit, believed in my work, and gave me terrific projects that allowed me to be very visible. If it wasn't for her, I don't know if I would have advanced so far in my career."

> A mentor is a guide, an advocate, a supporter, a confidant. If you enter an organization without connections, alliances, or family ties—as most Latinos do—you will need to be introduced and sponsored into the informal networks that are at the foundation of power in corporate America. Seek out a mentor at your company; there are many people out there who believe very deeply in giving a hand to qualified and dedicated men and women.

KNOWING WHEN TO CUT YOUR LOSSES

Alejandro has been trying to woo a client for several months. The franchising company where he works recently moved into the Hispanic market, and Alejandro's bicultural background convinced management that he was the right person to pull in more Latino subscribers.

But Alejandro is discouraged. He was sure he could convince a major Mexican American family-owned business to join up with his company. He has been spending most of his time at work writing and rewriting proposals and has been flying back and forth to Los Angeles to make his pitch in person. Alejandro realizes he is neglecting other potential customers because he wants to land this account so badly. But he is having a hard time letting go and accepting the possibility of failure.

Many Latinos find it very difficult—and not very *macho*—to admit to being wrong. Yet to advance your career, it is crucial to know how to cut your losses—to know the right time to admit defeat, walk away, regroup, and move on to a new project. An attitude like Alejandro's, of seeing the mission through no matter what, does not work very well in the corporate setting. In the business world, going down with the ship will not even earn you posthumous praise. Of course, the outcome of your assignments counts, but so does your judgment in completing them and your ability to see the big picture.

Things go wrong. People make mistakes. The truth is that nobody has ever made it into the executive ranks without goofing up or getting their nose bloodied.

> **It is not the mistakes you make that matter, but how you manage them. You can use a potentially negative situation to your advantage by demonstrating your decisiveness, flexibility, and willingness to turn missteps into opportunities.**

You have to develop the ability to determine when a setback is acceptable in your career and when it's not. You must also have enough self-awareness to recognize a pattern of mistakes.

> **Beware the CLM—the career-limiting move, a mistake that can derail your career in midtrack. The Hispanic executive has to be especially careful not to limit his or her advancement by appearing too ethnic or like an outsider. Once again, remember comfort and fit.**

You have to be strategic to avoid CLMs. Remember, CLMs are very different for Latinos and non-Latinos. If you do something to reinforce a stereotype—such as turn down a promotion because you don't want to relocate—you might never be offered another chance to move up in your company.

"You have to be prepared for opportunity," says Daniel. "If you come on too strong without knowing the ropes, you might appear not very intelligent.

"Let's say I go to my boss's boss without letting my boss know. That's political suicide, especially if I'm making waves over some sensitive issue. Chances are his boss will defend him and I will be out of a job. Or at least I won't have a prayer to get ahead in that company."

According to a study by the Center for Creative Leadership, 50 percent of executives whose careers derail before they make it to upper management show a lack of interpersonal skills.

> **Use the social aspects of your Latino upbringing to nurture and build relationships in the corporate setting.**

PLAYING THE GAME OF *LA POLITICA*

Unidad, lealtad, fidelidad. Loyalty is very important in the Latino community. We are loyal to our family, our friends, our colleagues, our companies, and our country. Our emphasis on loyalty is an asset in the corporate culture, because we are able to transfer our strong feelings of respect for those in authority to our organizations. We are deeply loyal to our sponsors and mentors for their role in our careers and for sticking their necks out for us. We are also loyal to our subordinates and peers.

You can't just have blind loyalty, however. You must be savvy about whom you go to bat for and whom you stick by.

> **In the corporate world—especially if you are Latino—you must learn to choose your battles carefully.**

You must decide what is important to you and how much you are willing to compromise.

You must study and absorb the *política* of your organization in order to succeed with your career advancement strategy.

Know Who the Players Are

Interpersonal relationships define and drive all organizations. Understand the hierarchy of your company. Become part of the informal network of the workplace, go out to lunch with your colleagues, ask them questions informally, exchange E-mail. Keep your eyes and ears open. Stay alert and absorbed. Know what's going on in your company, who's in and who's out, and who the people with power and influence are.

Overcome Your *Vergüenza* and Ask for Help

Even though Latinos are brought up to be interdependent, we don't place a high value on institutions. Thus we have a reluctance to seek assistance outside of our immediate circle. We feel that it is better to get through the rough spots on our own rather than rely on third-party intervention. We choose to suffer silently.

This is the complete opposite of how things are done in the business world, where favors are exchanged as common currency. Always remember the people who have helped you in your career and keep track of where they are. Offer them your help if they need it. And when you need it, ask for their assistance.

Take Carlos, for example. He works for a multinational investment firm. He is very eager to get an assignment in one of the Latin American offices but has not yet been able to get the coveted transfer, despite receiving high marks in his performance reviews. Carlos knows that getting an overseas posting is a key step in moving up in the company. He is frustrated that he has not been able to convince management to utilize his language abilities by assigning him to a Spanish-speaking country, where he would have the further advantage of understanding the local culture.

Carlos realizes that he is going to need some help to get where he wants to go. He does some research and finds out that a man for whom he had worked at one time and who was very friendly and helpful to him is now the manager of the company's Mexico City office. Carlos takes a deep breath and telephones his former boss. As it happens, the man is looking for an assistant manager and offers Carlos the chance to interview for the position. Not surprisingly, he gets the job—and a real boost to his career.

> **You can get help only by asking for it. Work to overcome the cultural inhibitions that stand in the way of your seeking out assistance and support from others.**

Learn How and When to Call In Favors

Just as you have to look to others to give you a hand in getting ahead, you have to be ready to help the people around you. This is not just altruism; you never know when you will need a return favor and who will be in a position to do it for you.

By the same token, you have to be sensitive and sensible about calling in favors. Think strategically. When you do something for another person, you build up goodwill. When you ask for something in return, you want to get the help you need without using up your goodwill capital.

Take Calculated Risks

Don't be defined by fear or a defensive posture. All your decisions should be made from a position of strength, or you will be sending the wrong kind of message to those around you. A well-planned, well-thought-out, well-studied risk is reduced to a marginal risk.

Don't Get Confused If Your Company Is Hispanic-Owned

It would be wrong to assume that the atmosphere of a Latino investment-banking firm on Wall Street will be more homey and laid-back than that of a company run by white males. Corporate culture takes precedence over the ethnic background of those in charge. If you think working for a Hispanic firm will be like hanging out with family and friends, you will not last long on the job. Corporations—like the armed forces—tolerate little or no differences in their ranks.

Respect the Diversity Within Your Own Company

If you want responsibility, power, and influence in your job, you must prove you can manage others. This means respecting differences and managing diversity. Keep in mind that while the decision makers in the organization might primarily represent the dominant culture, it makes sense that if we Latinos are employed by the company, our peers, colleagues, and subordinates will also be of different ethnic and cultural backgrounds.

Being a minority in an organization gives you an insight into what it feels like to be different. As a result, you should have a natural affinity for working with people who are different from you.

> **Executives who succeed have the ability to choose individuals with different skills and talents for their teams. Diversity is a source of strength and power—learn to be comfortable with it and capitalize on its richness.**

Benito, a Puerto Rican, is a top executive at a multinational communications corporation located in New York City.

"At the beginning, I thought I was going to pursue a public service career, not a corporate one. But I was hired right from college into a great company that came to my school looking for interested minority applicants. I was there a couple of years when I had the good luck to find a mentor. Really, she found me. As things turned out, because of management changes she became my boss. She was a woman who was very open and honest about what she knew and didn't know. I knew some things she didn't know, so she basically made an agreement with me, saying, 'Look, I'm going to show you the ropes and you show me what you know.' So it was great. It really worked out well.

"Today we've become best friends. She is very savvy in terms of what to say and who to talk to, when to talk, the best timing, how do you say it, how do you put it on paper. *La política.* Those things people coming into corporate have no idea about and unless someone tells you, you'll never know. Many times people don't tell you because they don't know you or because they don't care. When someone takes the time to show you, it can make a big difference.

"Another one of my first managers took the time after work to sit down with me and teach me basic writing and presentation skills. We would work together evenings and weekends. He was genuinely interested in helping people. And there are many people like that. If you ask, there are many people who are willing to assist you. After being helped by these two managers in the company, I was not afraid to ask for help from that point on. I saw that some people will say yes and some people will say no, but when they say yes, you win. You've got nothing to lose, but you eventually will win.

"Many Latinos are afraid to ask for help. We don't want to look stupid or set ourselves up for rejection. We don't want anyone saying, oh, this guy is uneducated or this guy is ignorant. We are afraid of being thought of as not knowing, so we don't take the risk. We want to maintain this image, and maybe it's because part of it stems from the overall general discrimination that we are exposed to. The stereotypes that Hispanics are not that smart or lack the proper education and credentials often hold us back from asking questions, even to an extent because we don't want to begin believing the stereotypes ourselves.

"Once we begin to get over the fear of asking for help, we can see that we have a lot to gain. You have to keep in mind that you can only get ahead by taking risks. Many times you don't know until you ask. For example, two weeks ago I went to the legal counsel of my company. I knew I wanted him to be my mentor and made an appointment to see him. I sat down in his office and said I would like to have his advice on various issues, some personal, some related to work. He seemed kind of surprised but also pleased that I was asking for his help.

"He started opening up. He told me that his wife was Hispanic and he had a special interest in seeing Latinos make it at the company. So, until you take the step, you never know. I have discovered that even people who are very, very busy will usually make the time to see you if you ask. That has been my approach and it's worked for me.

"My advice is:

> **Don't be afraid to ask; don't be afraid of being rejected.**

If someone turns you down, go on to the next person; you're the one who gains.

"My bullets for success are the following:

"One: Get to know your manager. Go out of your way to get to know him personally. Find out what kind of books she reads, what kind of sports he likes. What are her hobbies? This information will tell you a lot about that individual, not just how he or she is at work. You will understand this person on a more personal level.

"Two: Don't stay in your cubicle. Go out and meet folks around you. Establish relationships with your coworkers and get to know them.

"Three: Make sure you understand the company where you are working. Know how their products are doing, the extent of their stock, how it is distributed, and so on. Take the time, after work if necessary, to educate yourself about the organization. What have been their successes, what are some of the issues that are going on, how are decisions made. Don't be afraid to ask people who can help you understand.

"Four: Find a mentor. Find somebody who you won't be afraid to ask about things you don't know. Approach the person and say, 'I'm new here. Can I come to you from time to time and ask you some questions?' Most people will say sure.

Make the time to find mentors.

"Five: Do your job the best possible way. Particularly at the beginning because that will set up the base for your future path up the corporate ladder.

"Six: Don't be afraid to ask other Hispanics within your company for guidance and support. See if your company has a Hispanic Employee Association. Call them up, let them know you want their assistance. I remember the first time I came to my present company. At least once a week, someone from the Hispanic Employee Association here would call me. Benito, how's it going? Do you have any questions? Do you want to do lunch? It made a big difference, their reaching out to me.

"Seven: Network. At one point, I was a member of eighteen different associations. I was never home. But again, it was all part of my job. I also like that kind of activity. But, over the years, I've scaled back my involvement to two or three organizations that I can really focus on. Joining as many associations as you can, however, is invaluable. The people that you meet, the contacts you make, are essential for succeeding in the corporate arena. For example, I might call someone I've met through one of these professional groups to ask a question on a project that I'm working on. 'Here's that information,' I'll be told. 'We've just done a survey on it ourselves.' Boom—you don't have to reinvent the wheel. These networks and contacts pay off twentyfold.

"Eight: Learn to self-promote. Latinos are usually poor self-promoters. We are bashful about sharing the work we do. Our background emphasizes humility. I think that comes from our family, our culture, our upbringing. I mean, my great-grandmother used to say, '*No seas presumido*,' don't go around bragging. You will always be recognized if you do good work. In the corporate culture, this is the opposite: If you don't let everyone know who you are and what you do, you will get left behind. Of course there are some people who go overboard on this, but I think there are ways of making sure that management knows what you've done and the things you've accomplished. This is how it is in most corporations now because it is so competitive—unless upper management knows you were responsible for a particular achievement, you won't be considered a player when a career-advancing opportunity comes along.

"I was also taught that you've got to help others. *Tienes que ayudar, tienes que cuidar.* You must help out, you must care."

A LITTLE FAITH WON'T HURT

First you must visualize your success, then you have to pursue it. You have to believe that good things will happen and that you can make them happen. Your career advancement strategy must include faith, conviction, and determination.

"You not only plan for success, you also plan for opportunities," says Rosario, the New York bank vice president. "You can't lay out every step ahead of time, because you never know what will happen. The realization I'm coming to is that the higher you go in a corporation, the higher the stakes—your salary, your position, your chances for advancement. But you have to keep moving forward and take advantage of what comes your way. You can never stop believing in your dream and working to make it come true."

So will it help if your mother says her prayers? I like to think so. But keep in mind that the light of your mother's candles will not be enough to get you noticed in your job. Career advancement depends on the total package you put together, the whole enchilada: excellence in *performance*, the ability to create and promote your *image*, and your *profile* and visibility within the organization. And the light of the candles will help you find your way home no matter how far you get in your journey in the business world.

Career drivers are:

Performance
Don't just perform,
outperform.

Image
Similarity provides
comfort and fit.

Profile
Spread the word—
you do great work!

The demands that a career places on you and your family can be physically and emotionally draining. This is especially true during times of extended travel and tight deadlines. You know your family needs you, and you do your best to be there for them and still meet the demands of your job. If you get passed over for a promotion or you see someone less deserving move up, you sometimes question if it is all worth it. You drive harder to show yourself and your company that you have what it takes. You outperform and you make them take notice. You never, never quit.

—ZOE APONTE

ASSOCIATE DIRECTOR

THE REEBOK FOUNDATION

CHAPTER 8

CASA OR *CARRERA*

Reconciling Career and *Familia*

El que sirve a dos amos queda mal con uno.
One who serves two masters pleases neither.

Elena is looking forward to the family picnic she has planned for her husband and two children on Sunday. Late Friday afternoon her boss tells her that there's a sudden rush on the project they've been working on. It's now due on Monday, not Wednesday. They'll have to work over the weekend.

Elena knows that if she is to pursue her ambition of becoming an executive at her company, she has no choice but to work willingly through the weekend and miss the Sunday picnic. On the other hand, she also knows that her husband and children, not to mention *los abuelos, los tíos, los suegros,* and everybody else in *la familia,* will be disappointed and most likely regard her decision to go to the office as selfish and uncaring.

Meeting the demands of a successful business career and those of a meaningful family life is a central challenge for most executives in corporate America. Both career and family require time, energy, and commitment. And often obligations to work and home are at odds with one another.

The conflict between family and career is particularly difficult for Latinos who are determined to make it in the business world. Our culture places a great emphasis on the importance of *la familia*, and most of us grow up with a strong sense of loyalty not only to our parents, grandparents, and siblings but also to a wide circle of aunts, uncles, cousins, nieces and nephews, *padrinos*, and family friends.

Hispanic men and women who are devoted to their careers are subject to a lot of judgments by our traditional, family-oriented culture. Latinas often hear: "What man is going to want you if you are trying to be just like him?" "What kind of mother lets someone else raise her children?" "*Una mujersota*, a real woman, keeps an impeccable house and does it herself."

Hispanic men are equally criticized: "I am your wife. Why do you act like you are married to your job?" "You missed the birthday party because your work is more important to you than your daughter." "You leave your family all alone while you travel all over the country."

Latinos aiming to advance in corporate America must recognize the fundamental conflict between family and career and develop a personal strategy for dealing with it. For some, this might mean choosing to postpone starting a family. Others may decide on a career that leaves more time for a home life. Still others might try to have the best of both worlds.

Whichever way you decide to go, the key is to create a seamless whole, where your professional and personal lives are integrated and satisfying. Don't try to do a balancing act, but learn to blend your career and family as harmoniously as possible.

CULTURAL AND GENERATIONAL CLASHES

Most Latinos are raised to believe that there is nothing more important than the family and one's role within the familial structure. Yet for those of us who want to succeed in the business world, work and our standing in the company are a central priority. We feel pressured to abandon some of the basic values of our culture in order to fulfill our professional ambitions—and feel guilty as a result.

The way you go about reconciling your *casa* and *carrera* is very personal, depending primarily on your individual values and priorities. These are decisions driven by emotions, not skills and techniques. In earlier chapters, we discussed such topics as how best to prepare yourself for a career in corporate America, the importance of reading your workplace environment, recognizing and overcoming cultural stereotypes, understanding the unwritten rules and subtleties of the business arena, and accepting the values and paradigms of your organization. Yet if you do not reconcile your work and family life, it will be impossible for you to keep your focus and stay in the game.

To be successful at work, you must be at peace about your choices concerning your home life.

Latino executives have to contend with two major cultural expectations regarding family: traditional family structure and family loyalty. These can lead to both generational and cultural clashes that will affect the choices you make about your career.

Ironically, the traditional Hispanic family very much resembled the idealized Cleaver household of "Leave It to Beaver." Dad worked; Mom stayed home, took care of the kids, and cooked and cleaned for the whole family. In the afternoons, Mom would wait for the children to come home from school, then give them a hearty snack in the kitchen. At night, everyone would sit around the dinner table together, talking about what they had done that day. The only difference in Hispanic families was that there were more of us in the household and around the dinner table, because we either were brought up in an extended family or had relatives living nearby.

The "Leave It to Beaver" model doesn't work very well in today's society. The changes in the roles of men and women and in economic demands have redefined the way families function. Things are much more fluid and equal, with everybody pitching in and helping out. This new "family look" might make all the sense in the world to you, but you have to be aware that the break with tradition does set up a potential culture clash. Even the most successful Latino executives—those men and women who have been in corporate America the longest and have become very highly acculturated in the business world—are still often held back by the beliefs and opinions of their Hispanic upbringing. It is very difficult to turn away from the traditions and conventions of our *padres* and *abuelos*, especially when it comes to family.

The need to break with tradition sets up another conflict— that of loyalty. One of the core values of Latino culture can be summed up as, "*La familia sobre todo*, family at all costs." We say it, we preach it, and we truly believe it. But if you have career ambitions, you will constantly find yourself in situations that require you to put your work first, to try to balance, to compromise. The reality is that to succeed you have to be a team player. You have to be available when called upon to work extra hours, to travel, and to spend a great deal of time away from home.

You must be ready to confront the feelings of guilt about being "disloyal" to your family. And you have to be prepared for the reproaches you are likely to hear from the people around you. Your *tía* will tell you that you're neglecting your parents, your *hermano* will caution that you are traveling too much, your *abuelita* will comment that your children are looking skinny and underfed. *Poco a poco*, you might find yourself wondering if your relatives are right about your career choices and you're wrong. Remember, the powerful traditions of the Hispanic culture are deeply imbedded in our psyches, and you will have to face them throughout your career.

As a Latino aiming for the upper reaches of corporate leadership, you must redefine how you relate to *la familia* in light of contemporary American society and the current business climate. Do not let go of the core values and beliefs that ground you and help to maintain your balance, but adjust them to fit your ambitions and the corporate world of today.

WHAT DOES SUCCESS REALLY MEAN?

We Hispanics like to please. We want everybody to be happy and everything to run without a hitch. We want a high-powered, exciting career and a satisfying, intimate family life. This is very hard to pull off, though, and often you will have to choose between advancing your career and disappointing a person you care about.

You look at your accomplishments and say, "Hey, I received a promotion," or "I'm on the fast track," or "I've made it into the management training program. I'm on my way." You deserve to be happy and proud of your successes. But you also must recognize that the increased financial stability, professional recognition, and social standing these successes bring do not necessarily translate into your being able to fulfill the needs and expectations of others in your life.

Your promotion may mean relocating to another city; your raise may necessitate longer hours away from home; your acceptance into the management training program may mean more extensive travel. You must understand and accept *all* of the benefits, costs, and consequences of your moving up in the corporation. You then have to explain to your spouse, your parents, and even your children what your advancement will mean—for you and for them.

For example, if you grew up in a family where no one has even left *el barrio*, the neighborhood, what happens if your new position requires you to relocate halfway across the country? Or even to the other side of the world? How are your parents and in-laws going to feel about being far away from their grandchildren, not to mention their own son or daughter?

Your career decisions have a direct impact on those people who are close to you. Therefore, all the potential consequences of a more impressive title and increased responsibilities need to be discussed and analyzed with the members of your family. "Do you know this means my moving away from home?" you might ask your mom. "I'll be working sixty-hour weeks," you may have to tell your husband. "I won't be able to coach your Little League team anymore," you might need to tell your daughter.

Sacrificing family commitments for the sake of career advancement is not for everyone. And after weighing the pros and cons, you may decide that certain requirements for a new position are unacceptable. "I can't travel more than two days a week," you might say to your boss; "I really don't want to relocate," or "I would prefer not working every weekend."

By the same token, if you decide not to work weekends or enroll in that marketing course, you may begin to feel frustrated when your peers are promoted into higher management positions while you tread water. You may start to harbor resentments against your family. "I wish my spouse could be more understanding," you may think. "I wish I had more support," or "I wish my children were not so attached to their cousins and friends."

Unless you bring these conflicts out into the open, whether with your employer or your family, you will always be on the defensive, afraid that you're letting someone down. And sooner or later you *will* let someone down if you don't discuss these issues, confront them, negotiate them if needed, and finally accept them. And that someone will be you.

You should discuss the relationship between your career and family on a regular basis with people close to you, and there should be enough flexibility and understanding to incorporate changes and compromises. The emphasis the Latino culture places on *la familia* impacts every issue in the *casa* vs. *carrera* conflict:

- Should I get married?
- Should I have children?
- Should I get outside child care?
- What happens if I travel frequently?
- How do I explain to my children when I miss their birthdays and school plays?
- How can I deprive my parents and in-laws of seeing their *nietos* grow up?
- How can I move my family away from our relatives, friends, and community?
- How can I live in an area with few or no Hispanics?

Don't try to juggle the deal and figure out how you are going to please everybody, because you're not. Some people are bound to be disappointed and hurt by your decisions—in both your home and your workplace.

To climb the corporate ladder, you must make sacrifices in both your *casa* and *carrera*. Since there is no one successful model for everyone, you must create one that satisfies your particular needs. Maybe you'll have to choose to work in a family-friendly company that has time sharing for its employees or day care on the premises. Perhaps you will choose to marry a stay-at-home spouse who accepts and supports your travel schedule and crazy hours. Or maybe you'll reprioritize your career goals and ambitions.

> **You must clearly understand your personal and professional needs and work to blend them together.**

Every person in corporate America faces a similar set of challenges regarding family and career. Yet because the Hispanic culture is traditionally very family-oriented and close-knit, we are less geared to relinquishing our attachment and commitment to our immediate family, as well as our *tíos*, *suegros*, *hermanos*, *sobrinos*, and assorted *parientes*. In the mainstream culture, for example, when you hit eighteen, boom, you're out of the house. Yet the majority of Latinos this age—even college students—are still living with their parents. And it is not considered unusual or unhealthy.

Your dedication to making it in the corporate arena can often trigger feelings of guilt or discomfort about your obligations and duty to *la familia*. Do not attempt to change your core values, the ones that have made the Hispanic culture strong and rich with tradition. Instead, reevaluate and readjust your priorities in light of the contemporary business environment and learn to blend the best of our heritage with your contemporary lifestyle.

WHAT'S BEST FOR YOU/WHAT'S BEST FOR YOUR FAMILY

You're tired from coming home every night at ten. You missed your son's soccer game again last Saturday morning because you had to go to the office. You've been asked to accompany the vice president of marketing on a two-week business trip to South America to meet with the top business leaders of the continent; the only problem is that you'll be out of the country for your tenth wedding anniversary.

In preparing for your climb up the corporate ladder, you might have told yourself that your family would always come first. Now that you are becoming a successful executive, you find yourself questioning how you got so caught up in this crazy deal that is demanding most of your time and energy, forcing you to put your family's needs in second place.

But then you hit on the big contradiction. As you examine your motives for pursuing your professional goals, you remember why you got into the game in the first place: to be a good provider for your family. You want to give your kids the opportunities you never had—a certain type of living environment, economic stability, educational possibilities, and growth potential. You want your children to grow up with wide horizons and unlimited access to people and places. You work as hard as you do to offer them advantages you never had because of financial limitations.

> **Your professional success does put your family first by providing those you love with a secure present and a promising future.**

Our parents' generation may not understand our willingness to change, especially if we appear to have a comfortable lifestyle.

Marcelo, a senior-level executive in the packaged food industry, recently accepted a position at a new company. He calls it a dream job. With a significant increase in responsibility and compensation, it seemed as if the job description had been designed and written specifically for him.

There was only one drawback. The new position was fifteen hundred miles away. Although Marcelo had not been actively seeking a position outside his company, he was always open to listen when executive recruiters contacted him. He would share with them his two requirements. First, he would never consider a lateral move. What would be the point? After all, his company had been good to him. His career was progressing at a satisfactory pace. Professionally and financially he was currently satisfied. Therefore he would only entertain leaving if the move meant a major professional growth opportunity. Second, Marcelo would not consider anything more than a hundred miles from home. Relocation was out of the question.

All this changed when he started discussing his new position. It was too good to pass up. An opportunity like this might not come around again. He would accept. But Marcelo would not relocate his family. They were tied to their home, extended family, friends, schools, and community. It was decided that Marcelo would commute. He leaves home Sunday night and returns on Friday. Weekdays in one city, weekends in another.

When Marcelo shared the news with his father, not unexpectedly the announcement met with some resistance. "*Hijo*, aren't you doing well where you are? Don't you have a good position with some seniority? You make such a good living. You have a beautiful, big house in a wonderful neighborhood. My *nietecitos* attend the finest schools. You take vacations. Why would you give this up to spend the weeks away from your children?

"When I was young I had to leave my home and family behind to find work and survive. I had no choice. I had no schooling. I suffered and made sacrifices, working day and night, so that you and your brothers and sisters would have a better life than me. You went to school so that you would not have to do what I did and not suffer the same hardships as I did. I don't understand, *hijo*, but you know what's best for you and my *nietos*. *Dios te bendiga*, I give you my blessing."

Marcelo realized something ironic that day. *Los viejos* have taught us that if we go to school and prepare ourselves for a professional career, then we will spare ourselves the hardships that they endured. Our culture teaches us that it is the responsibility of each generation to secure a better life for their children, the next generation. In the eyes of our *antepasados*, one of these hardships is displacing family to seek or follow opportunity.

In the mainstream corporate culture, however, it is totally acceptable for educated professional people to put themselves through the same hardships that our parents try to spare us: moving from place to place, working long hours, extended business travel, and time away from family—in essence, being corporate migrant workers. The irony is that here it isn't a hardship—it's a privilege. It's called advancement.

The upward climb is hard work! It's long hours, it's compromise, it's meeting a multitude of demands. It is pursuing professional growth outside of the office. A promotion might mean taking a course at night or putting in some extra hours of reading before you go to bed. If you're the type of person who wants to get home, leaf through the newspaper, watch television, or help the kids with their homework all evening, then maybe you should reconsider your career goals. You don't get ahead in business without really trying.

As I mentioned earlier, there are also social and civic obligations required for recognition and promotion within your organization. If you buy into the blending model, you can use these business-related activities as tremendous opportunities for your family to be exposed to new experiences and adventures.

What it boils down to is your being willing to reevaluate the definition of family and what it means to you within the context of your professional life. Then you must confront those issues that create conflict, whether with your spouse, your children, your parents, or your extended family. You need to engage in a dialogue through which everyone will understand the demands of your career and either get on board or admit that your ambition is incompatible with your family life.

You must be cognizant that some tough decisions will have to be made. Ideally, everything will blend smoothly, and you can have a satisfying personal life, a fulfilling family life, and a rewarding professional life. But if this doesn't happen—or doesn't happen harmoniously—be prepared for the fact that sacrifices may have to be made.

> The higher up the corporate ladder you go, the more essential it will be for you to know how to negotiate compromise between family and career and to make difficult choices.

MALE PRESSURES/FEMALE PRESSURES

For most Latinos, the tension between *casa* and *carrera* is defined by how heavily we are invested in the traditional notion of an "ideal" family and our roles in it. And although the conflict of family versus career is a central issue for all Hispanic executives, men and women encounter different sets of conflicts and pressures in the course of their professional pursuits.

For men, the struggle tends to be to find a happy middle ground between the traditional role of provider and the reality of the modern family, in which both spouses are likely to work and share domestic responsibilities. The "Leave It to Beaver" paradigm of yesteryear no longer works. This in itself can pose a threat to a more traditional male Hispanic. But even for those Latinos who have no problem with their wives working, the need to give 100 percent at work and be a partner in raising the children and running the house is a tall order.

In today's global business environment, a corporate executive can be sent halfway around the world at the drop of a hat, missing birthdays, family outings, and other significant occasions, and generally not holding up his end of the bargain. This can quite naturally create a lot of tension between husband and wife, and parents and children, especially if the family has not openly discussed the relationship between career and home.

A man's capacity to participate fully in the raising of his children is an especially delicate issue. A father's connection to his sons and daughters has to be nurtured with time and patience—a difficult thing to do if you are working eighty-hour weeks and spending half of your free time on business-related social and community activities. Yet with careful planning a father can participate fully in his children's lives.

"When I'm gone I'm all business, but when I'm with my kids I'm all dad," says Bernardo, a sales representative from Miami. "I love what I do. My work fulfills me and makes me more complete as a person, which in turn makes me a better partner and parent. I work hard and play hard, and ultimately this will benefit my kids. I don't think I'll regret my current decision to blend my family and work somewhere down the line. As a matter of fact, I'm sure I'll be glad for it."

Latinas who choose to pursue a career in corporate America

face a whole other set of problems and stresses. In the Hispanic culture, there is a very specific image of what a woman should be—a
wife and mother—and how she should act. A woman who concen-
trates on her work flies in the face of tradition and is considered
"incomplete."

A Hispanic woman who opts to pursue her professional goals,
especially in the demanding world of business, will hear such comments from her more conventional friends and relatives as: "Who
gives the kids their breakfast?" "How do you feel putting such a
young child in day care?" "Can you trust a stranger to clean your
house?" All these veiled criticisms say the same thing—that the
woman is being selfish and neglecting her family.

"I get a lot of flak from my grandmothers and aunts about
spending so much time at the office," explains Laura, a marketing
consultant from San Antonio. "I tell them I'm working such long
hours because I want to provide my daughter with all the economic
advantages I never had. My salary makes it possible for her to
attend the finest private school in the area and to take ballet classes
and clarinet lessons.

"Even though I'm not at home as much as my mother was
when I was growing up, I believe I'm just as devoted a mother as she
was to me. My suegra tells me that I should apply for a civil service
position, where I would work nine to five. 'Get a real job,' she
urges.

"What really saves me is that both my parents are very supportive of my career choices. They have encouraged me every step
of the way. They have acknowledged my independence and drive
from day one and have never tried to influence me to change my
course."

And what happens when a Latina makes a conscious decision to delay having children or to have none at all? "You mean
I'm not going to see my grandchildren before I die?" your mother
will cry. "You'll be sorry for your decision when you find yourself too old to start a family," your sister will warn. A Latina who

chooses not to have children because she's pursuing a professional career will get pressure not only from her immediate family but also from virtually every woman in her extended family and her community.

Even with this pressure, there are more and more Latinas who are not even considering marriage, let alone having children. In their decision to go after their ambitions, they face intense scrutiny and skepticism from the Hispanic community.

"When I got my last promotion—the highest for any woman in my company—my wealthy *tío* in Costa Rica called me and asked, 'When are you going to quit playing around and get a real life?' " laughs Dora, a record company executive. "By that comment, he meant when was I going to get married and have kids. In our culture, if you're a single woman, it doesn't matter how successful you are. You are defined by your husband and children. But I can't let that bother me. If I did, I would lose my edge in business.

"I've reached that point in my career where I'm just as ambitious as any man. I like being in the game, although the concept of competition is different for men and women. If men fall, they may get angry, but they get right back up and in there again. When women stumble, we get more introspective. We doubt ourselves and start questioning where we went wrong.

"When this happens to me, I wonder if I made the right choice about putting off having a family. I hear my mother's voice in my head cautioning me that time is running out, that I'll be turning thirty-five next year. But if I start letting myself think like that, I'll lose my momentum or, worse, my competitive edge. So I have to put those doubts out of my mind."

The irony is that our elders have always encouraged us to get good educations and solid jobs in order to become part of mainstream America. They want their offspring to enjoy a life of economic freedom and professional opportunity, to have the advantages that were out of reach for them. Then, to a certain degree, once these goals are accomplished, they sabotage their messages by trying to pull us back to the way *la vida* used to be. "We wanted you to get educated and have a career and all that," they say, "*pero no tanto*, not *that* much."

Under the blending model, every member of the family is aware of the enrichment and fulfillment that is derived from the different aspects of one's life. The professional part is just as important to being a whole person as is the personal, the social, the civic, and so on. You need to communicate this openly and honestly to your spouse, partner, or children, and you have every right to have your view listened to and respected.

> **The people in every part of our life must respect the importance that the other part of our life carries. If not, you may find yourself facing conflicting values and having to make decisions accordingly.**

The reality is that if you decide to pursue a career in corporate America, you will face a myriad of pressures from both your family and your peers. Although Hispanic men and women must deal with a different set of issues, each of us must face breaking with some of the traditions of our Hispanic upbringing as we climb the corporate ladder.

> **It is up to you to be a trailblazer, to create a new model for Latinos that successfully blends family and career, without weakening the strong fabric of our community.**

MARITAL PRESSURES

While there are individual problems that male and female Latino executives must face, clashing careers can cause great stresses within a marriage. Let's say you have an educated couple, both husband and wife on fast career tracks. All of a sudden one gets a promotion and has larger professional demands placed on him or her. And the other person is left with less companionship, a larger share of domestic responsibility, and probably growing resentment.

Why is there such strain? It's the old tapes coming back to haunt us, telling us what a wife or husband *should* be. If your wife has to put in extra hours on her job, working evenings and weekends, for example, you might start feeling abandoned. After all, your mother was always around the house when you were growing up. And sure, your sister works, but she's a teacher and is able to be home by four in the afternoon.

Or maybe your husband is on the road four days out of every week. You are left behind to organize and run an entire household, in addition to working at a full-time job. Where is the equity in this arrangement? you find yourself wondering. He comes home for the weekends, and everything is already taken care of. You have to compete against his work, almost as if his job has become his lover.

Careers and relationships require strong commitment and a lot of work. In a partnership between two people dedicated to their professional goals, there will invariably be times of friction and shifting balance. It is essential that you communicate with your partner about your ambitions and your frustrations. Together you will have to devise a strategy for meeting the demands of your family and your careers.

> **Trying to have it all requires a realistic appraisal of what can and cannot be accomplished and a unity of purpose and action.**

BLENDING FAMILY AND CAREER

Most of us resist the idea of making our family too structured or having it run like a business. We grew up with the attitude that work is out there, *beyond* the door, and that our home life should be all warm and fuzzy, full of love and harmony. Unfortunately, in this day and age, a model such as this doesn't always work. Contemporary American society requires you to organize your personal life with the same precision you plan your business day.

To begin with, the members of your household or intimate circle must be informed about your career goals and the sacrifices you are prepared to make to achieve them. You should explain to them how far you want to advance in your professional life and what you think it will take to get to where you are going. You must also make it clear to your family how you think your sacrifices will impact their lives.

You must then devise a strategy to keep the family functioning at a level that is acceptable to all members. Parents and children alike should know what is expected of them, how they fit into the picture, and the exact goals and objectives you are setting for yourself. Once your plans are laid out, they should be reviewed on a regular basis.

In order for you to achieve a successful blend of work and family life, your whole family should be intimately involved in your career. It no longer works to say that you can't or won't bring your work home with you. You'd *better* bring your work home, otherwise the distance between your two worlds will only increase.

There will be some marriages or partnerships that cannot withstand having one or both individuals involved in a high-stress, demanding career. Therefore, choices will have to be made. Perhaps a career—or relationship—will be lost somewhere along the line. There are no right or wrong answers. You must be aware, however, that as you climb the corporate ladder you will face conflicting priorities every step of the way.

If blending your career requirements with your family obligations becomes unrealistic or impossible, you may consider leaving the corporate world altogether. Or you can take a less demanding position within your organization, one that does not require as much time and energy. If your job is jeopardizing the stability of your household, you may choose a career track that doesn't provide as much economic growth but gives you more time to maintain your emotional equilibrium.

Only you can decide whether or not it is worth the many sacrifices and adjustments necessary to reconcile the demands of your professional pursuits and those of your personal life. Make no mistake about it: A successful career creates a great deal of strain, and a family that is not well equipped to handle such stress will break from the pressure.

"PLANNED SPONTANEITY"

One of my early bosses told me how he used to hold family meetings every Sunday evening. He explained that he, his wife, and his children would discuss their plans for the upcoming week and figure out what they would be doing and when. Then they would all open their planners, go over their scheduled appointments and activities, and decide which were flexible and which could be changed only for a dire emergency.

I told him that it was the oddest thing I had ever heard. But what's more, it seemed so cold and mechanical.

"You know what?" he answered. "You seem to me to be a loosey-goosey kind of guy. Real spontaneous, you know, doing whatever feels good at the moment. You don't want to disappoint anyone. You want to keep everybody at your house happy and everybody at your work happy. Even though you're fine about organizing a game plan at the office, I bet you feel that if you were to do this kind of planning with your family, it would take something away, make you seem like some kind of machine."

"You're probably right," I reluctantly conceded.

"The funny thing is," he went on, "that as a result of my being this way, I have more time to be spontaneous than you do. Because if I don't plan it out on both the professional and personal fronts, I will always be scrambling. And in my running around, I'm bound to screw up somewhere. Something will fall through the cracks.

"I know exactly what's going to happen on a day-to-day, week-by-week basis," he went on. "As a result, I can carve out more time to spend with my family. By being structured, I am more accessible. I call this *planned spontaneity*—blocks of time when I can do whatever I want."

Planned spontaneity. Just hearing the words used to drive me nuts. It sounded like a contradiction in terms, like some kind of weird tongue twister. But now I understand and incorporate this philosophy into my own life.

> **Good planning—professional and personal—allows for more free time.**

SINGLE PARENTS

Alejandra is a success by anyone's standards. She dropped out of college in her second year to work in retail sales after the birth of her daughter, thinking that her husband would finish school first and she would go back when he graduated and started his career. When her marriage ended, Alejandra was determined to finish her degree to be able to provide her daughter the best possible life. It wasn't easy being a full-time breadwinner, full-time student, and full-time mom. Many times she thought of quitting, but how could she look at herself in the mirror? How could she ever face her daughter?

Throughout this challenge, Alejandra relied on a loving support system: parents, brothers, sisters, *tías*, and *abuelos* all willing to baby-sit, cook meals, and help with laundry. She couldn't have done it without them. Graduation day was especially meaningful to the entire family.

Now Alejandra is a human resources manager. It is hard, satisfying work, but it is not where she wants to be. There are better growth opportunities in other areas of the company. She has often been interested when things have come up; other times she's been approached with career possibilities. The only problem is, in her company most of these opportunities require relocation.

Alejandra doesn't feel she can do that. Not now, not with her *hijita* so young. Alejandra feels tied to her support system. So for now, she'll watch opportunities come and go. She knows sooner or later they'll stop asking. She gets frustrated; sometimes she gets resentful. But she just keeps working, convincing herself she's doing the right thing.

If the demands of corporate life put strains on traditional families, they doubly stress the single parent. Many single parents feel trapped in dead-end, unrewarding jobs because they do not feel they can take the risks associated with change. Others, like Alejandra, feel tied to a geographic location because of their reliance on family and friends.

Single parents must learn to manage their careers as they would a business. Opportunities must be weighed on the basis of individual merits and their relationship to your overall career strategy. Few opportunities come without a downside or trade-offs. You will therefore need to be open to alternative, creative, or nontraditional solutions to these obstacles. Remember, if you always do what you've always done, then you'll always get what you've always gotten.

Don't paint situations with a broad brush. Make informed decisions. Consider all options objectively before accepting or discounting any. You may conclude that you cannot under any circumstances take the risks. Your decision might then be to stay put or seek opportunities outside your organization that do not require you to leave the community.

FAMILY-FRIENDLY ENVIRONMENTS

The ideal solution to the problem of reconciling *casa* and *carrera* is (1) share the importance of your work with those closest to you, or

(2) find a position in an organization that is supportive and sympathetic to your personal and home life.

If you have children, you should make an effort to talk with them and communicate how Mamá or Papá is healthier and happier because of the stimulation and challenges you find in your work. "Work is *not* a drag," you should explain to them. "It's exciting and exhilarating. I do it because it's *good* for me to do it, not because I have to." Think of the important message you are sending your children with these words!

In addition, more and more companies are becoming family-friendly, and if this is important to you, actively look for career opportunities in organizations that truly value the importance of family.

"I work in a company that not only stresses how important home life is but also encourages its employees to become involved with their respective communities," says Alberto, an executive at a San Francisco accounting firm. "In a practical sense, what ends up happening is that each division within the company is managed by an individual who sets the tone for how things run. And if you're lucky—as I am—your boss's values will coincide with yours. I work for a man who leaves the office early to attend his child's basketball games. His actions determine the office culture for the rest of us.

"It also depends on how willing a corporation is to enforce its stated values. The company's philosophy must begin at the top and trickle down through the ranks. My organization has always been particularly involved in community activities and philanthropic pursuits.

"I started a program tutoring inner-city Hispanic children in mathematics, which became very successful. The chairman of my firm found out about this from the employee newsletter and called me to his office to congratulate me. His recognition sends a specific message to my peers—and supervisors, too—that the management encourages this kind of involvement.

His praise makes all the long hours I put in on the job seem worthwhile."

> **Know yourself, know your family, and know your career goals, so that you can blend your professional and personal lives. In charting your climb to the top, keep your objectives in harmony with the realities of your personal commitments and family responsibilities.**

You can't balance;
you'd better blend.

Planning and communication
are your best allies.

Sometimes you have to
make tough decisions.

As you progress in your organization, your profile in the community also grows. You will be called on to represent your company and participate in organizations and events that are of strategic or philanthropic importance to the company. Some of these events might be in the Hispanic community, others may not.

Inside your organization you may be accused by some of self-promoting. In your community you may be perceived as becoming detached. It comes with the territory. Never apologize for your success. Be proud.

—SARA R. GARZA GÓNGORA
SOUTHWESTERN BELL CORPORATION

CHAPTER 9

LIVING THE AMERICAN DREAM LATIN STYLE

Spreading Salsa on Your Piece of the American Pie

Llave de oro abre cualquier puerta.
A gold key opens any door.

Not too long ago, I was traveling in Mexico with a group of top U.S. executives, researching a joint venture opportunity. One afternoon, between meetings, I took my American colleagues on a tour of an upscale residential neighborhood in Mexico City. As we drove past the beautiful large houses with their manicured lawns and magnificent gardens, several of the executives commented on the fact that groundskeepers were tending most of the homes.

Later in the day, during dinner, we told our Mexican partners about our excursion, and it so happened that one of the senior members of the Mexican delegation lived in the neighborhood we had toured.

"We noticed a lot of people working on the gardens," said one of the U.S. executives. "Do you have a groundskeeper?"

"Certainly. In fact, several," the Mexican executive replied. "I like my residence to look as impressive as possible, and fortunately I can afford to pay someone to keep it up."

There is a common thread among people of affluence that crosses cultural barriers: a big house, private schools for the children, season tickets for the local sports team or the opera, membership in the country club, luxurious vacations.

Is the Mexican executive living the American dream? Is he living the Mexican dream? The answer is both.

> **The dream is success; the dream is empowerment; the dream is influence; the dream is prosperity. The dream is economic and social well-being. The dream is not limited by cultural and geographical boundaries. The dream is the same all over the world.**

Successful executives, regardless of their ethnic origin or cultural background, share remarkably similar lifestyles once they achieve a certain level of professional and economic recognition. Membership in the corporate hierarchy not only determines your status in the office but also defines your social and civic standing in the community.

> **Your lifestyle is determined more by your success than by your culture.**

The more successful you are and the higher you rise within your organization, the more latitude you are allowed in your behavior, especially regarding the very cultural differences that set you apart from the other executives in the first place. Most successful Latinos skillfully blend their Hispanic and corporate identities to enjoy the best of both worlds. As they acquire greater power and authority within the corporate structure, the issue of their Hispanic background diminishes in importance and significance.

In addition, once you reach high leadership levels, your values and priorities will have a significant impact on the paradigms of the organization as a whole. Because you are now in a position to set the standards for your company, your views can help pave the way for other Latinos to be promoted into upper management.

THE CULTURE OF SUCCESS

Success is its own culture. But success is not only about money; it is also about lifestyle. Take a professional athlete, for example. A high school basketball star goes to college on a full scholarship. Maybe he graduates with a degree, or maybe he leaves school in his junior year to join the pros. He signs a multimillion-dollar contract and becomes an instant financial success. He now earns the same amount of money as a CEO of a major company. But his lifestyle is completely different, because he is defined by a very different culture.

The corporate culture dictates what are acceptable and unacceptable sets of behaviors, leaving only enough room for slight variations in individual style.

"I'm a wonderful French cook, but I always throw in a Puerto Rican dish when I entertain," says Lisa, a senior executive at an insurance company. "I feel secure enough now in my career to let my guests know about my roots—and my mother's recipes!

"At the many business functions I attend, very small portions of the same kind of bland food are usually served. It seems almost required. So when I have people to my house, I try not to call too much attention to myself by going overboard with plates and plates of spicy foods. But the higher I rise within my company, the more adventurous I'm letting myself feel. It's almost as if I'm trying to push the envelope to see how much cultural diversity the corporate hierarchy will tolerate."

The higher you climb in the organization, the wider your sphere of influence grows. As a result, a paradigm shift takes place, with your values becoming models for the people who work for you, your peers, and even the rest of the organization. The Latino emphasis on family, for example, can influence company personnel policies to allow for flexible hours and time sharing. Or you can help institute formal mentoring programs for local students.

How do you know if you have achieved the American dream? When are you an "official" success? Your climb up the corporate ladder began with your setting specific objectives for your success. Yet goal setting means different things to different people. Along the way you have set certain standards and benchmarks to measure your progress relative to your intended destination. Your success is defined by how close you have come to reaching your goals.

"One of my first lessons in corporate America was that there is a great distinction between the organization and the individuals working there," says Martin, an executive with a national restaurant chain. "It doesn't matter if the CEO of your company is Anglo, Latino, or African American. He represents an organization with its own culture, mission, and purpose. And the basic purpose of any business is to make a profit. Therefore, when I approach my senior-level colleagues with a plan or an idea, it is my responsibility to contribute to the ultimate goal of the organization, to the bottom line. If I don't do that, I am not acknowledging the goals of the company and the reason for its existence. And I'm failing in my personal mission of being a strong corporate leader."

Success is very subjective. Some of you might measure your achievements by your economic security, others by the acquisition of material objects. For others, it will be the status and recognition you receive from your peers, your community, and society at large. You must ask yourself what you consider to be important. Is it getting your name in the paper? Is it buying a brand-new car every year? Is it establishing a scholarship for Latino youth in your parents' name? Is it being quoted on television as an expert in your field?

Each of us has different hot buttons, different things that excite us. It is not the same for everybody. But it is critical to know:

- What you want and when you've gotten it
- How to measure your success
- How to make your lifestyle reflect your achievements and accomplishments

Being successful and living the lifestyle of success doesn't mean you've sold out and are being unfaithful to your upbringing. It doesn't mean you're living "white." It means you're enjoying the fruits of your position and wealth. The manifestations of your accomplishments are the common threads that run through the lives of all successful executives.

Is the American dream the same as the Latino dream? Yes, because it is the dream of success. When people fantasize about what they would do if they won millions of dollars in the lottery, their daydreams about how they would spend the money are very similar, regardless of their cultural or racial background: "I'll buy my mother a house; I'll travel around the world; I'll put my children—and nieces and nephews—through college."

But hitting the jackpot or winning the lottery is very different from achieving a set of goals you have carefully worked for over many years. You don't become the CEO of a company by buying a ticket or feeding quarters into a one-armed bandit.

> You have been working steadily and carefully your whole career. By the time you get to where you want to be, your lifestyle will be a reflection of the years of hard work.

LIVING THE AMERICAN DREAM

María was a business consultant in Los Angeles who specialized in Hispanic clients. Her seminars were very pro-Latina, and she was very proud of saying that she "reeked of Chicana." She wore her hair slicked back and always dressed in extremely bright colors. Her pitch was, "This is who I am—who we are—and they have to accept it. We can't let anyone tell us that our heritage is not as worthy or exemplary as theirs."

Eventually María was hired to work as the chief affirmative action officer for an international communications corporation. She succeeded in opening up the company to a large number of minority employees. She was recently interviewed in a major metropolitan newspaper, and her photograph showed a woman with a completely different look: She was wearing a conservative business suit, her hair was short and smartly styled, and her makeup was subdued. *María was wearing the uniform.*

So did María no longer "reek of Chicana"? And what did that mean, anyway? At a certain point in her career, it was important for María to be very extreme in the way she showed her Latino heritage. In her current position, she's showing her Hispanic roots in a different way—by helping to provide access to corporate employment for qualified members of her community and by serving as a role model for her people.

The truth is that you should not be afraid that you have sold out or have forgotten your Hispanic heritage just because you drive a nice car, live in a large house, or have many of the material possessions people aspire to. You own these things because you can afford them. They do not change who you are or where you came from.

As Norman Vincent Peale says: "Have absolutely no guilt about being happy and successful if you operate honestly and with a sense of social responsibility."

"Even though I am totally comfortable in the corporate culture, I'm always aware of my Latino upbringing," says Daniel, the California communications executive. "When I'm at work, I act a certain way. But when I'm at home or with my friends, I enjoy music, food, relationships with my family, even the language of my upbringing.

"I always stress to young Latinos who are intent on climbing the corporate ladder that in order to succeed they have to play by the rules. And it's very simple: Those with the power are the ones who establish the rules. You cannot impose your rules—or your culture—on corporate America. When you reach a certain level of achievement, however—when you become the boss—you can begin to make certain changes and to assimilate your values into the organization.

"You can't create change by walking away or by moaning or complaining. You create change by being successful and influencing the people around you. For example, I have more than a hundred people reporting to me. When we have meetings, I get up and talk about the value of diversity. My staff look at me and think, 'Hmm, he would like it if I could put together a diverse management team.' So the next time a position in their unit opens up, they're more likely to hire a person from a different background, with a different point of view.

"I have made a concerted effort to blend my corporate life with my Latino background. I feel comfortable driving to work in my blue suit and red tie and listening to Mexican music on my car radio. I believe I have a responsibility to myself, my family, and my community to be successful, because I know the more visible I am, the greater the impact I can make on people's lives.

"For me, achieving the American dream is about being accepted. Spanish was my first language, and this always made me feel like a second-class citizen. Being considered an American and not a foreigner is very important to me. My success also enables me to provide a good life for my family and have the financial security to make sure my children receive the finest education available. In addition, I am now in the position to help other Latinos also make their dreams a reality."

In the 1980s, we heard about trickle-down economics; now we have trickle-down diversity. By our successes, we can turn the trickle to a mighty river.

"Once you're in a position of responsibility within a company, you realize you have the opportunity to impact your value system on those around you," says Benito, the communications executive from New York. "For example, I have my real *familia* at home and my family at work. In both places, I think of each person as part of a team. My wife and children have a stake in my career and help me in fulfilling my obligation to my employer by being flexible about my hours and work responsibilities.

"At work, we are also a team. We are all working to get this product out the door, and we do whatever we have to do to make it possible. Wherever I have worked, I have developed a close relationship with the people there. I get to know them, they get to know me, and this has helped me in being successful. Because we all pull together when times are hard and celebrate together for a job well done. At work I like to create a synergy of *familia*.

"I believe in loyalty and caring, both in your personal and professional lives. For example, if one of my employee's kids is sick, I say, hey, go take care of your child. If your mama is sick or your grandma had to go to a doctor's appointment, take care of her because I know it will come back twofold.

"At some point, however, you have to watch out for yourself. *Cada quien que se las rasque como pueda.* I've reconciled to the best of my ability the hard task of having to fire someone who works for me, for example. I think of how I can place those people somewhere else, in another area or another company. I consider the options and I know I can start calling my network to find a job for that person. So I make that transition. But it is not an easy one. But in the end, I must own the responsibility for my action.

"The responsibilities of senior management are not easy. Any time you have to terminate someone involuntarily or lay them off, it's always tough because you are talking about another person's livelihood. So it never becomes easy for me just to say, you're out of here. I have to help the person move on. Those are my values."

"My mother worries about my losing my job when she hears all this debate about cutting out affirmative action programs, even though at this point of my career I'm not affected by it at all. She gets confused and upset. Every time I change jobs, always to higher-paying and more responsible positions, I might add, she asks me why I would risk the present stability for the unknown. '¿Mi hijito, por qué vas a dejar ese trabajo?' Why are you leaving this job? What are you doing? Stay where you are.

"She calls me and tells me to pray. Then she lights a candle to her favorite *santo*. I know she worries, so I try not to go into too much detail with her about my work. The studies say we are going to change jobs four, five, even six times in our careers. But our parents came from a generation where you stay put. Any change is a potential risk."

"What does success mean for me? From a financial standpoint, success means being able to buy the things that I could never buy, my new Mercedes 450SL, for example. It means being able to provide things for my daughter and my wife, things that they want. To dress nicely and not have money always on my mind. This comes from the earlier stages of my life, when I was barely able to afford one pair of tennis shoes a year, if that. Because that was all we could afford.

"Success also means being able to reach a level of professionalism where I feel secure and proud. It is having a job where I can make decisions and have an impact on others. It is also being able to travel and take trips and visit places. Because growing up we never thought we would be able to go to Paris or other countries; there was just not even an idea of it. Being able to see the rest of the world, that is success."

CULTURAL COMFORT AND EASE

A Latino community group in Dallas is planning a street festival to raise money for a training program for disadvantaged Hispanic youth. The group is looking for corporate sponsorship and approaches Ernesto, a junior manager at a Fortune 100 company.

Ernesto grew up in the very neighborhood the program serves. Although he believes in this group's work, Ernesto is hesitant to ask his boss to intervene with senior management to sponsor such an event. He is afraid he will be viewed as someone whose loyalty lies with the Latino community and who gives ethnic issues higher priority than the goals of the company.

Miguel, a Cuban American, is the chief financial officer of a major oil company located in Dallas. When he is approached by the same group for corporate sponsorship for its festival, he quickly approves the request. He knows that supporting such a cause would improve his company's relations with the Latino community in the city. Because he is a top executive with a proven track record, he is secure in the knowledge that his decision will be viewed as one that is based on solid business policy and not on cultural allegiance.

Hispanics living the American dream integrate the strengths and vision imparted by their upbringing with proven strategies for succeeding in the business world. By blending their Latino and corporate cultures, they have acquired—and currently enjoy—positions of power in this country's economic hierarchy. *De un éxito nacen otros éxitos.* Success breeds success.

Once you achieve status within your organization and economic prosperity, you can be more flexible about following the corporate rules.

All the little details you worry about while on your way up become nonissues once you get to the top of the corporate ladder. On reaching the level of top management, you enter a small, closely knit circle whose members don't merely tolerate but rather support and protect each other.

As you climb through the ranks you must concentrate on assimilating into your surroundings. By the time you make it to the higher levels of the organization, your adaptation to your company's culture has already become internalized, and you've started operating on automatic pilot. You already know how to dress, how to decorate your office, how to speak in the appropriate manner. Therefore, some variations in your behavior are more easily accepted within the context of your organization's culture.

"I now have some paintings by young Hispanic artists hanging in my office, along with the requisite prints of ducks and ships," says Marcelo, the food company executive. "I was very careful to avoid promoting 'ethnic' art when I was at a lower level, because I didn't want anyone to think, 'Look, you can never really take "them" out of the *barrio*.'

"I'm also in a position to recommend funding projects to strengthen the company's involvement in the Hispanic community, so we can increase our share of the Latino market. When I was an entry-level guy, if I had proposed giving even five hundred dollars to the Hispanic Chamber of Commerce, for example, the response would have been, 'Come on, get with it. You know, there's more out there than just Hispanics.' Now my suggestions are viewed as wise marketing strategy.

"There's no doubt about it—the higher up in the organization you go, the more you can get away with. When you become a player, you earn the privilege of rank.

"Like most other Hispanic executives, I had to make the climb on my own. Many of my colleagues attended the same colleges as their boss or were part of the same social set. Take golf, for example. Some of these guys here have been on the golf course since they were five years old. Well, I could throw a mean curveball, but I had never seen a golf club when I started work. So in order not to lose the opportunity to network, I went out and took golf lessons. Now I'm a fine player and sought after as a partner by many of the other top executives in my company. I don't see this as selling out or becoming 'white.' Instead, as in all areas of my work, I try to fit in, so that I am not different from my coworkers.

"I have worked very hard to maintain a competitive business edge that was not given to me as a social or economic birthright. At

this point in my career, I feel very comfortable with the choices—
and concessions—I have made in order to succeed in corporate
management."

Success is also the perception that others have of you. A few
months ago I met Orlando, a Hispanic executive on the fast track
at a major beer company. He had recently been transferred to Milwaukee from Atlanta, where he had lived in a predominantly white
neighborhood. He decided that his children had been missing out
on some important aspects of their Latino heritage and that it
would be important for his family to live in a Hispanic area of
Milwaukee.

Orlando and his wife went house hunting the weekend before
he started work, and they discovered a vibrant Latino community
in the city. He was very excited—there were nice homes, friendly
people, bakeries, food stores, churches, and so on.

When he started his job the following Monday, his coworkers
asked him how he had spent the weekend. Orlando answered that he
had been out looking for a place to live. Everyone began making recommendations: "Most of the executives in the company have houses
in such-and-such development. But you can basically live anywhere
you want—just stay the heck away from the north side of town."

Well, the north side of town was exactly the Hispanic section
where Orlando had decided to purchase a home. The area that had
excited him was considered the most undesirable part of town by
everyone at his office. In the end, he ignored his coworkers' advice
and moved his family to the Hispanic neighborhood. Orlando was
senior enough in his company to get away with it. Because of his
position, he was allowed slightly more leeway to live in an area
somewhat off the beaten track—and one that called attention to
his Hispanic culture to boot.

Orlando's example is a fairly unusual one, however. If you get
used to a certain lifestyle or are expected to use your home for business functions and entertaining, you probably won't find an appropriate half-million- to million-dollar house in the *barrio*, no matter
how hard you look.

> **In the corporate world, where you live reflects your professional and economic success, usually leaving little or no room for individual tastes and cultural diversity.**

COMMUNITY INVOLVEMENT

Hispanics in senior management positions blend so smoothly into the corporate culture that they are indistinguishable from other CEOs and company presidents. Yet when these high-achieving men and women are invited to speak to professional Hispanic organizations, they serve as very powerful role models. They don't talk about driving the bottom line at their companies or about strategic planning; instead they give inspirational presentations that urge other Latinos in the corporate arena to continue their quest for entry into the upper levels of management. They point with pride to their humble beginnings and tell about the strength they derive from their Hispanic upbringing.

> **These successful businessmen and women add the Latino flavoring to the American pie.**

"I now feel comfortable serving on the board of directors of predominantly Hispanic organizations," says Andres, the Mexican American chief executive officer of a national brokerage firm. "At first I wanted to be associated only with groups that benefited the American public across the board and were not ethnically defined. But now I realize I can lend my name and the prestige of my office to help the Latino population—especially the youth—of this country.

"By example, I'm also getting my employees to become involved in nonprofit groups and community organizations. I believe in giving back and sharing the dream. In my current position of power, I can impart this philosophy to hundreds or even thousands of people."

Like Andres, if you've made it to the top of the corporate ladder, there will be many nonprofit and community groups pursuing you with offers to join their boards. How should you choose? To begin, remember that the reason for your success in the business world is most likely your skill at managing your career in such a way as to create a broad-based constituency. You must bring this inclusive vision to bear on how you choose to become involved with the community. For example, you should not concentrate exclusively on Hispanic causes and neglect the rest of the population. Instead, you should take an interest in a variety of umbrella organizations and charitable foundations, in addition to smaller groups that promote Latino issues.

Let's say you're not yet a CEO but are still making your way up through the ranks of corporate leadership. Obviously your success up to this point shows you are not one-dimensional but have a varied set of interests. Therefore, you are probably cultivating a diverse set of activities, some ethnic, some social, some cultural, some artistic, and some driven by a need to progress in your career.

If you see that the American Cancer Society is the pet project of the top person in your organization, for example, politically it would make sense to become involved in this particular cause. This would probably be a smart career move.

Yet let's say your true interest lies in music, and you would like to raise funds for the local symphony orchestra. In addition, you would like to participate in a tutoring program for Latino youth. Taking into consideration the constraints on your time, you have to make a choice.

You end up going with the American Cancer Society, because it's the right thing to do for your career, and the tutoring program, because you feel the need to give back to the community. The local orchestra will have to wait for now.

Your choices reflect your personal and professional priorities.

When can you start spreading salsa on your piece of the American pie? Once you feel financially and professionally secure, you can begin to enjoy the kind of freedom that allows you to be more selective about your outside interests. Because of your time limitations or for political reasons, you may choose not to join a certain board of directors officially but serve instead as an honorary member. In this way, you can lend the prestige of your company to a grassroots or community-based organization. You may also opt to support groups or programs you care about by donating funds; you can even do so anonymously. You can become a patron, establish scholarships, or work with your company to offer summer internships for qualified students. You will soon discover that there are many creative ways to reach out to the Hispanic community.

"One of the most satisfying perks of my position is the time I am allowed to spend tutoring Hispanic children in the community," says Rosario, the New York banking executive. "It's very healthy for me to be around these bright young people, who are the future of our Latino community. These kids not only teach me patience, they also reconnect me with my heritage. I have always carried my Hispanic roots around on the inside; lately I've found myself wearing my heritage more openly on the outside. My growing comfort level with my Latino background, even in the homogeneous culture of corporate America, reconfirms that I have made the right choices in my career path."

MAKING INFORMATION-DRIVEN CHOICES

The climb up the corporate ladder is all about choices. All along the way, you are constantly making decisions and revising your plans.

> **Your decisions, however, are only as good as the information you possess.**

How you process your accumulated knowledge is up to you. Only you can determine the negotiables and nonnegotiables of your career advancement strategy and make the value decisions that will determine the course of your career.

> **When you take a risk, even if it's well thought out and well studied, it is still a calculated gamble at best. It is a leap of faith.**

Many Latinos who are striving to succeed in the business world grew up in the homes of parents who had limited educations. We have had scant exposure to corporate America. Most likely we are the first in our families to graduate from college and pursue an executive career track. As a result, we don't have the ready access to the inside information of the corporate arena that some of our colleagues enjoy.

> **We have to run harder to keep up. We have to study more, work longer hours, volunteer for everything. We have to overcome educational and social hurdles and absorb all those subtleties and unspoken rules that nobody told us about.**

My friend Joe, a Cuban American, was sent to the Detroit office of a major food manufacturing company. After four years there, he finally asked his supervisor why the organization had stationed him in Detroit for such a long time.

"Because you're a minority," was the response, "and there are a lot of minorities in the city. We thought your background would work in your favor."

Joe wanted to answer, "Hello, I'm Cuban. If your goal is to reach a specific minority population, send me to Miami." But he knew his company's reasoning was that Detroit had a big minority population, and that's all. The corporate brass didn't get into the subtleties of ethnicity. African American, Latino—there was no big difference to them.

Instead of getting angry, Joe got smart. He researched the buying power of the Cuban American population in Miami, drew up a marketing plan to reach this influential minority, and submitted his ideas to his boss. On the basis of his proposal, Joe was sent to open a Miami division of his company, which quickly became one of the organization's leading moneymakers. As a result of his success in Miami, Joe received a series of promotions. He is now third in the chain of command for the entire organization and is working out of the company's headquarters in Memphis. In his present position of power, his being a minority has been rendered irrelevant and inconsequential!

Living the American dream does not dilute your Latino legacy. You are just getting your piece of the American pie and pouring salsa all over it. *Mi casa es tu casa,* and my success is your success. *Bienvenidos,* and welcome aboard!

Enjoy your success; you deserve it.

Success is color-blind.

With success comes commitment.

I always want to keep a sense of who I am and remain close to the humble nature of where I came from.

This is sometimes a challenge when you obtain financial success. It is also a benefit. It shows that goals we set for ourselves are achievable. I can be a role model and show that you, too, can reach and obtain.

I am involved with a variety of organizations that help me give back to the community. Being in corporate, we must realize that we can contribute to the community in many ways. We can be the voice of the community and promote awareness. We can educate in both directions, coaching our community on how to deal with corporations and promoting the community in the boardroom. We can role-model and mentor.

This responsibility requires active participation. Always ask yourself, "How am I doing? Am I doing as much as I can do? Am I helping others? Am I making a difference?" Because of all the demands on your time, when it comes to your responsibility to the community, you may not always be as accessible as you'd like to be; you may not be as in tune as you should be. But look always within yourself and make sure that you never lose your commitment.

—FRED R. FERNANDEZ
DIRECTOR OF EEO AND
WORKFORCE DIVERSITY
UNITED PARCEL SERVICE

CHAPTER 10

IT'S ONLY LONELY AT THE TOP IF NO ONE ELSE GETS IN

Now It's Up to You to Be the Mentor

Hoy por mí, mañana por ti.
Today for me, tomorrow for you.

When I first moved to Denver, I had a supervisor whom I'll call Steve. A couple of days after I started in my new position, Steve asked me to pick him up at his home. I arrived promptly at seven, as we had agreed, in my Volkswagen convertible—a car I loved and considered almost a member of the family. Steve came out of the house, got in the car, and we started off.

We exchanged some polite small talk, and as part of the conversation Steve casually said: "Nice car. It's something my kids would drive."

I got the message loud and clear. The next day I traded in my beloved VW for the biggest four-door, corporate-gray Buick I could find. I knew that even though I had lost an old car, I had found a new mentor.

That was more than fifteen years ago. Recently I met an executive who had just been promoted to senior vice president at the same company. In the course of talking about our careers, I mentioned Steve and told the story about the car. He began to laugh.

"Juan, you won't believe it, but the same thing happened to me," he said. "It was my first day of work, and Steve asked me to pick him up at his house. I had a souped-up Chevy, with a jacked-up rear end and racing tires. Steve got in my car and gave me directions to the company headquarters, or so I thought. All of a sudden, we were in front of the Lincoln dealership. Steve took me directly to the general manager and said, 'Fix him up. I'll cosign if I have to.' "

As we continued to compare notes, we realized that Steve had been a generous mentor to both of us. He had shown us where to bank, pointed out suitable neighborhoods in which to purchase a home, and advised us on the right attire to wear to fit in at our company. Steve took the time to show us the way. And I'm sure he helped plenty of others like us over the years.

Once you've made it to the top of the corporate ladder, you should always remember how you got there: people who helped you, doors that were opened for you, colleagues who invited you into their offices to fill you in on the real story, and supervisors who stuck their necks out for you. And you must be prepared to give those coming up behind you a helping hand in advancing their careers. Your success takes on a whole new meaning when you share it by being a mentor or a guardian angel for others striving to make it in the business world.

As we Latinos enter leadership positions, our sphere of influence becomes wider, and we come to have a meaningful impact on our community and society as a whole. As a result, it is also very important that you lend support—both personal and corporate—to local and national Latino youth and educational groups, community organizations, arts councils, and social service agencies.

> Your success makes you a significant role model for other Hispanics. You are now in a position to mentor others into upper management positions within your organization and to assist young Latinos who are looking to join the ranks of corporate America. Just as someone helped you on your journey, you must extend yourself to others who are pursuing dreams of success.

A MENTOR IS THE KEY TO SUCCESS

To be an effective mentor, you have to understand the nature of the mentoring relationship—what a mentor can and cannot do. The best way to learn mentoring skills is to be mentored yourself and to make note of the sort of help that made the biggest difference for you. Then give the people you want to help the nurturing that you most appreciated.

No matter what you do, having a mentor often makes the difference between isolation and invisibility and professional recognition and growth, especially for Latinos. Success doesn't happen just because you do your job well. It also requires networking, developing political acumen and leadership qualities, and learning the art of self-promotion. A mentor is critical in helping to hone these skills and to develop corporate savvy.

- A mentor serves as a role model, a nonjudgmental counselor, or a trusted sounding board for work-related problems or ideas.
- A mentor shows you the ropes, decodes the organizational culture for you, and guides you through the thicket of office politics.
- Mentors act as a buffer between you and senior management.
- Such an individual advises you on how to position yourself for career advancement and leadership growth.
- A mentor brings your talents to the attention of people in positions of power and provides access to crucial professional networks.

> **A mentor should not be considered a savior who will take care of all your problems; rather, he or she is someone who can help you utilize your talents for maximum career growth.**

What type of person is best suited to be a mentor? There are some people who are naturally inclined to coach and teach. You should seek out individuals who truly have a desire to share their knowledge and experience. And when your time comes, you should also ask yourself if you are suited to be a mentor. Do you have what it takes to provide this kind of nurturing to others?

Over the past several years, many organizations and companies have introduced formal mentoring programs. These are often race- or gender-specific approaches that are meant to ensure that every employee has the opportunity to be mentored and to mentor others. Be forewarned: These structured mentorship programs are sometimes not well planned, successfully implemented, or monitored carefully. For such programs to work, management must be held accountable for their effectiveness. Unfortunately, in many instances this is not the case.

If you work in an organization with a formal mentoring program—whether you are the mentor or the "mentee"—you should make sure there is a strict accountability for its success. These types of structured programs succeed only if they promote mentoring as a way of providing equal access for each employee. This in turn makes the whole company more productive and a more rewarding place to work.

"My first mentor was assigned by the company," explains Osvaldo, a vice president of a major hospitality firm. "We had formal weekly meetings, where he basically would ask me if I had any questions, and I would be too nervous to reply. We gradually lost all contact with each other.

"In the meantime, I was studying at night for my MBA. The senior manager who had to sign my vouchers for school began to notice me. One day he saw me reading a copy of the *Wall Street*

Journal during my lunch break. He commented that I was a real go-getter, and I could see that he was impressed.

"The next week, he invited me out to lunch. He said that he was putting a team together to work on a new project and asked if I would be interested in coming aboard. I could barely stop myself from shouting, 'You bet your life!' He explained that he couldn't help everybody but that if he could help two or three people with their careers, he would consider himself fulfilled.

"My mentor—or *padrino*, as I often thought of him—told me that it is easier to lend a hand to people who want to be helped. And I made it clear I wanted to be helped. I wanted to be part of his team and make his project a winner. *Cada uno poniendo su granito de arena*. I wanted to do my part for the group.

"Although my mentor was not Hispanic, he was a first-generation immigrant, just like me. So, because of our backgrounds, we had a lot in common. We both knew the value of hard work, of making it on your own, of being raised in a family where you are the first to graduate from college. We just clicked on every level.

"Really good mentors don't go around just trying to duplicate themselves. Their actions aren't purely altruistic; there's also a self-interest there. My mentor's primary goal was to create a team that would work well together and make money for the company. It just so happened that the best way to achieve this goal also helped the team members grow as individuals.

"Joining my mentor's project was the beginning of my ascent within the firm. This generous man not only encouraged my work, but he also made sure that those in high places were aware of what I was doing. He had faith in me, and I didn't want to let him down. I was working for myself, but I was also working for him. He's now retired, but I would still do anything for him."

If you are being mentored—or choose to be a mentor—the first thing you need to do is define what the relationship means to you. Oftentimes *informal* mentoring is most successful. You can find informal mentoring opportunities through networking, by joining associations, or by attending events sponsored by professional groups and employee organizations. These give you the chance to interact with others in your field, to exchange information, and to build contacts.

In looking for a mentor, do not limit yourself just to other Hispanics. Look at every executive at your company as a prospective mentor. Select a person from whom you can learn those skills you want to develop and eventually pass on to others.

It is important to be familiar with people from all races and cultures. For example, a white professional can offer an insider's perspective on the organizational norms and culture. An African American mentor, on the other hand, can give you hints about succeeding as a member of a minority group.

If you do choose a mentor from the predominant culture, be careful to evaluate his or her comfort level with racial and ethnic issues, including any assumptions and expectations he or she might have regarding Hispanics.

Remember, mentoring is a two-way street—it's not just about getting promoted. When you choose a mentor, you should expect to reciprocate that person's trust in you. Once you and a mentor agree to pursue a relationship, you need to sit down together and put your individual expectations on the table. Decide how you want to get together, if you want the relationship to be formal or informal, where you would like to meet, if you should see each other on a regular basis, and what you would like the relationship to accomplish.

"The key to my success was having four different mentors at different points in my career," says Daniel, the communications executive from California. "I had good people coach me, give me solid career advice, open doors for me, and create opportunities for me. If it weren't for them, I'd probably still be spinning my wheels in the same place. That's the way things are in the corporate world."

Mentors are usually individuals who have attained a certain level of success in their organization. On their journeys, they have undoubtedly stumbled and even occasionally lost their way. Their experiences of making mistakes along their career paths can provide invaluable lessons. By pointing out the pitfalls they have encountered, mentors can help others to avoid them. "I don't want you to make the same mistakes I made," is the message. "This is what happened to me. Don't let it happen to you." This is a very important part of the mentoring process.

No matter who your mentor is, *you* are ultimately responsible for your own decisions and career advancement strategy. Take the case of Manny, for example. A middle manager in a Fortune 500 financial services firm, Manny started with the company in a regional office. Eventually he was assigned to implement a major nationwide initiative in his region.

Manny had reported directly to the regional senior vice president who had brought him to the firm, but because of his new assignment, he now also reported to the individual at corporate headquarters who ran the national initiative. His relationships with both of his supervisors were good. His performance ratings were always high, and his region always ranked among the best in the company. Manny felt that he was fortunate enough to have two powerful mentors.

The firm then reorganized, and Manny's regional senior VP was reassigned to corporate headquarters. Manny was part of the team that went with him. The assignment the team was given was a transitional one, with no guarantee of a permanent position at its termination. Manny was not worried. He had already survived the initial cut, and surely senior management would find him a spot. Hadn't they already brought him to headquarters? His senior VP had taken care of him by including him on the team. He just had to keep performing, and he would be okay.

What Manny didn't realize at the time was that the senior VP was positioned to be let go at the end of the assignment. One of his two mentors was on his way out.

Manny then found out that his other mentor was considering retirement. He was led to believe that he was the heir apparent for the vice presidency. The retiring VP told him that he was the logical choice, that because Manny had been so successful with the initiative at the regional office, he could step into the role and the project wouldn't even skip a beat. The VP promised to schedule the necessary interviews. Manny felt good. Not only was he going to keep his job, he was going to get a promotion.

Time passed, and no one said a word about an interview. The VP was to retire soon, and there was silence about the position. Manny asked occasionally but never got a clear answer from the people upstairs. Finally, shortly before he was set to retire, the outgoing VP told Manny that senior management had settled on another candidate.

"But I never had a chance to interview," Manny complained.

"I didn't think you needed to, since everyone on the committee knew you," was the VP's reply.

The truth was that no one knew Manny. They knew of him from reports, but that was it. Manny realized the mistake he had made: He had placed all his faith in his mentors rather than taking charge of his own career. He had transferred to headquarters during a power shift and had not networked or connected with the new administration. This group saw him as an outsider. By remaining tied to two departing executives, he was identified as part of the old guard.

Manny learned two valuable lessons from this experience. He found out that names and numbers on reports don't get promoted, people do—people with whom those in charge feel comfortable, people who fit in. He learned that unless you have access to the decision makers, you won't have a chance.

Manny also saw the importance of reading the corporate environment. He had the help of two individuals, two people who had thought highly of him and had been good to him in the past. But Manny had the wrong people carrying his message. They were individuals with no audience.

Manny didn't learn the politics at headquarters. He never bothered to find out who was "in" and who was "out." As a result, Manny found himself "out." He did, however, learn an important lesson about mentors.

> **Always carefully read the environment of your organization, especially when you choose your corporate mentor.**

GUARDIAN ANGELS ARE ALSO WELCOME

Guardian angels take the mentorship relationship one step further. They not only give you information and show you the ropes, they also look out for you on all levels of the organization. Guardian angels advise you on the political implications of your moves and decisions, protect you, pave the way for you, speak up on your behalf, and stay on the lookout for anything that might derail your career.

> **A guardian angel *protects* in addition to coaching and teaching.**

"I was lucky to have a guardian angel from the start of my career," says Rosario, the New York bank vice president. "She helped push me up the chain of command. She gave me projects and allowed me to prove myself. She was really terrific about bringing my work to the attention of the right people. She went out of her way to help me at every step.

"The worst thing that can happen to you as you climb the corporate ladder is that people stop sticking their necks out for you. You need individuals to vouch for you. Your guardian angel will step up to the plate for you. Sometimes it feels as if you're getting preferential treatment—almost like being the teacher's pet, in a sense. But my guardian angel was smart enough to understand this and knew exactly what to do. She didn't make our relationship obvious or blatant to my colleagues.

"We have a very businesslike relationship. We don't socialize outside the office or even go out for lunch together. But I know I can see her anytime, anyplace, and talk to her about anything.

"What we have in common is that we're both resilient. I think that's why she identified with me and decided to help me out. She has advocated for me throughout the years, and I have a strong sense of responsibility to perform well for her. Loyalty is very important in our culture, and I know I will be loyal to her for life.

"Now I'm at the point in my career where *I* am both a mentor and a guardian angel to others. It's a big honor but also a big responsibility. The majority of the people I've mentored are Latinos, African Americans, and women. I feel that now I'm able to give back, and it makes my work even more worthwhile and important."

THE LEGACY OF OFFERING A HELPING HAND

There is a Chinese proverb that says: "If you plan for one year, plant rice. If you plan for ten years, plant a tree. If you plan for life, educate and teach."

A child taking its first step or saying its first word is a source of great joy and celebration for parents and grandparents. But what if after taking that first step, the child sat down and never took another? What if after uttering that first word, the child never spoke again, thinking there was nothing more to say or do? Would there be a similar cause for joy and celebration?

The same can be said for the success that any one of us may achieve. If after reaching our goals we stop our journey, deciding that there is nothing else to do—if we never coach, mentor, or help anyone else along the way—is there really any reason to celebrate our accomplishments?

Una mano lava la otra mano, y las dos lavan la cara. One hand washes another, and the two hands together wash the face. Any Hispanic man or woman who makes it in the corporate arena—or in any other arena, for that matter—has an *obligation* to guide other Latinos along the same path that led to his or her own success.

You must always look at your accomplishments in a historical context, from the perspective of the struggles of the people who came before you and paved the way for your successful journey. You should never forget that there are important legacies that need to be honored. There are many individuals who made tremendous sacrifices to help the Latino community prosper and progress. Many doors have been opened. But there are more to open, and if we are to continue to thrive, we must make sure that as many people as possible keep coming in. Every person who enters those doors opens them a little wider for those who follow.

> Once you have attained your goals, do not make the mistake of believing that you did it on your own. As I mentioned earlier, while there may be self-made failures, there are certainly no self-made successes.

It is imperative that you, as a Latino, try to bring more and more of our people onto the road to success. You must share with members of the Hispanic community those skills, strategies, and ideas that will enable them to reach for and achieve their goals.

WHY SHOULD YOU MENTOR?

"I truly believe that it is important to be able to give back, to make things better for other folks who are coming behind," says Benito, the communications executive. "I know that whenever opportunities have come my way, it was because someone along the line has always helped me. Therefore, if I can help one person at a time, then it will make it easier for someone else and someone after them. The help will keep spreading.

"When I first came to this country from Puerto Rico, I didn't know a word of English. I was put in school, and I knew the kids were making fun of me because I couldn't understand a thing. I sat in the classroom and read, read, read. The other kids would tease me all the time. The worst part was going out to the playground. I would sit by myself and listen to everyone laughing at me.

"One day this kid—I'll never forget him—took the leadership of coming over to me and talking to me. From that point on, he took me under his wing. He basically told the other kids to lay off and stop making fun of me. But he also included me in the group's activities. And when that kid took that leadership role to help me, it made the whole difference. If he had not, I could not have gone on. I may have quit. I remember him all the time and reach out to others because I know how it feels to be empowered by friendship and support."

Hispanics have a heightened sense of community. Ours is a culture that is based more on collective aspirations than individual ambitions. And that makes us good mentors.

Mentoring enhances two communities, the corporate and the Hispanic. An organization is strengthened by its managers' commitment to developing individuals for leadership roles within the corporate structure. Companies that promote from within attract and retain the best talent by communicating to their employees that management recognizes and rewards ability and dedication.

For the Hispanic community, mentorship provides access to educational and economic opportunities. If you are willing to bring people along with you on your climb up the corporate ladder, you will be furthering the goals of our people by helping as many others as possible integrate into mainstream society.

Mentors have a strong desire to share. Whether they coach young people in athletics, act as peer counselors, tutor, or extend themselves in other ways, mentors nurture, impart information, and give freely of their time and knowledge.

When I first joined corporate America, I quickly realized that there were very few people who shared my cultural background. I was greatly influenced by the people who mentored me throughout my career, because they really showed me the value of sharing. So one of the things I did—and this is a personal decision that each of us needs to make individually—was to search for ways I could mentor and help other Hispanics.

I decided to conduct presentations and workshops to reach a large number of young people. I wanted to connect to the next generation of Hispanic leaders, coaches, and mentors. I decided to work with youth groups, college leader forums, and organizations of young Latino professionals. With each presentation, I learned something new and felt more rewarded by the respect of the bright young people whom I met.

> **The mentor is as enriched as the person being mentored.**

The first mentor I had in my life was in Mexico. He had a team of people who worked with him, and we were all almost like his children. It was a family environment. His entire senior staff—there must have been twelve or thirteen of us—started the day by having breakfast together at his home. We ate around this huge table and then rode to the office together in a motorcade.

Our boss counseled, coached, and advised all of us individually, and also held collective advice sessions around the conference table in the office. So it was very different for me when I entered corporate culture in the United States. I quickly found out that mentorship was more one-on-one here. But what was clear to me, and what remained etched in my mind, was that mentorship, whether individual or collective, has to be ongoing to be worthwhile.

Consistency is vital in developing a productive mentoring relationship. It doesn't matter where you rank in an organization; you must have a deep interest in developing people. You can be a mentor at any stage in your life. When you're in high school, you can mentor grade school kids. When you're in college, you can tutor high school students. In your company, you can give a hand to others who are looking to improve their status within the organization.

As you go along on your journey, there will always be someone else following you. Mentoring is a way of guiding others by providing road maps to those paths that you have traveled. It is sharing information about what to expect on the road: the location of the potholes, what exits to avoid, the best time of day to travel, when to rest, when to stop to reflect, when to forge ahead.

> **It is always the right time to mentor. You can always share what you know about the portion of the road you have already traveled.**

The decision to mentor is extremely personal; it is not for everyone. In the business world, it is easy to become focused on "me." There are those people who will say: "Hey, it cost *me* a lot of trouble to get here. Nobody ever helped *me*. I pulled myself up by my bootstraps. Let everybody else do the same thing." Yet this can be a very self-defeating attitude, because ultimately people who think this way find themselves alone.

Some people are threatened by mentoring others. They feel that if they help a talented person develop, that person will end up taking their job. If you are afraid that the people you nurture will eventually outgrow you, most likely you won't be a mentor. Mentors have to be secure enough not only to assist others to fulfill their professional, intellectual, and technical potential, but also to provide a platform for the launch of a new generation of individuals and executives who have the ability and capacity to surpass their mentors' achievements.

If you choose to be a mentor, you have to do it in the spirit of wanting to see those people you help achieve even more than you have accomplished. But you also have to pass on to them your conviction that each generation owes it to the next to pave the way. Only then will we have the progression of growth within our community that is essential to our continued success.

MENTORING IS ALSO GOOD FOR YOUR CAREER

Like parents who want to ensure that their children have better opportunities than they have enjoyed, mentors need to grow individuals who, in turn, will grow the organization. Executives who develop people who contribute to the company in significant ways are recognized by management as important assets. They are viewed as confident, progressive, and visionary.

Mentors who are good developers of talent are seen as putting the goals and objectives of the organization first and looking out for what's best for the organization. Mentors are considered important to making the organization more successful and profitable and are valued for that reason.

As a corporate insider, you have access to the culture of your organization. You are therefore in a position to bring people in and to coach them about that culture.

"I mentor because I don't like to see a person's potential going to waste," says Rita, an executive with a leading software company. "There are too many talented people out there who should be given more of a chance. It's especially important to let young people know that there's a world outside the neighborhood; that it's not so bad wearing a tie or looking outside the *barrio* for a job.

"I feel a responsibility to educate and help out these kids, because I know firsthand how difficult it is for a person of our background to compete in the business world. But mentoring is also good for organizations. It shows that corporate America has an interest in a diverse group of people and is flexible enough to include different points of view."

HISPANICS AS MENTORS

When high-level Hispanic professionals introduce other Hispanics into the management pipeline, it not only enhances their own viability as leaders but also ensures that they will no longer be so lonely at the top. Yet the mentoring process does not have to be limited only to providing access to your own corporation; you can also use your organizational resources to mentor young people or help people who are seeking careers in other sectors of corporate America.

Among the perks and privileges of success is the opportunity you have to affect our community. By achieving a certain level of power within your place of business, you are in a better position to reach out to other Latinos. A common stereotype of Hispanics—and to some degree of minorities in general—is that we have a greater loyalty to our ethnic group than to the organizations where we work. This perception (or misperception) can often stand in the way of our being promoted and moved into senior management positions. But by participating in the politics of your organization, by blending into its culture, and by achieving concrete, bottom-line-driven success, you have dispelled that false notion of exclusive loyalty. You are seen as a team player—an individual who has the interests of the organization at heart—and therefore are able to mentor and promote other Latinos without raising the suspicions of your colleagues.

However, you must be able to demonstrate to upper management that your outreach to the Latino community is valuable to the organization. This includes developing new markets, cultivating a pool of talented individuals who will contribute to the company's profitability, and creating goodwill among the local Hispanic population.

Your success makes you a role model in the Latino community. Your influence is not limited to your corporate commitment but might extend to mentoring—through example or personal involvement—men and women who work in areas such as education, civil service, or nonprofit organizations. There will be some aspects of coaching and mentoring that are unique to your company, however, specifically those that deal with the unwritten rules and unspoken codes of your organization.

Every organization has a culture, and your success in climbing the corporate ladder is based on your ability to identify, understand, and navigate your company's specific environment. Therefore, it is especially important that as a mentor you communicate, transfer, and help develop those skills that pertain to your organization.

There are many other messages that you can pass along as part of the mentoring process: for example, the importance of continued professional development, the value of education, advice on how to read the workplace environment, and so on. This information can apply to people working in any industry, not only to those who are in the corporate world.

The fundamental principle to keep in mind is that you do not have to limit yourself if you are going to be a mentor. As a Latino, you should be cognizant that you are participating in developing a new generation of leaders. And these leaders are going to exercise the skills you pass on to them in a variety of areas, in a variety of ways, in a variety of situations, in a variety of environments.

It can sometimes be intimidating for young people to approach individuals who have attained a certain level of success. They automatically assume that they cannot have access to you.

> **You should take any and all opportunities to share information with others and let them know that you are there for them.**

Information can be shared in any setting, from formal business meetings to recreational events. Your influence as a role model is often very subtle. All it might take is for you merely to attend an event, where someone looks at you and says: "You know what? I don't know too much about you, but I would like my professional life to resemble yours." Maybe it's the way you dress, the lifestyle you seem to have, the respect you seem to command. Your very presence communicates to other Hispanics that there are many career options open to them. And that in itself is a form of mentoring.

Do not overload potential "mentees" with information. We all have to crawl, and then walk, before we start to run. Offer advice appropriate to a person's position. Let's say Steve is a junior in college, looking for a summer internship at your company. He sees you at your son's school basketball game and asks your advice about how to go about getting the internship.

Your dialogue could go something like this:

YOU: Have you applied for the internship yet?
STEVE: Not really, but I'll be starting pretty soon.
YOU: Well, you know, don't wait too long. This is the time the company starts reviewing applications. Have you ever interviewed at a corporation?
STEVE: Yes, I went to XYZ Company.
YOU: Let's talk about the interview. How did it go? What kind of organization was it? What did you

see there? How did you act during the interview? Did you feel you fit in?

STEVE: To be honest, I thought they were just doing it as a formality.

YOU: Why is that?

STEVE: I don't know. I just didn't feel the interview went that well.

YOU: Do you know anybody who got a position at that company?

STEVE: Yes, I do.

YOU: What was it about *them*, do you think, that was different from *you*? Did they dress differently, did they study different things in school, have they had different community involvements, do they know someone inside the organization?

Most likely Steve will have picked up valuable advice and guidance from this seemingly casual conversation. Your questions have probably shaped his future course and given him a focus for some basic career decisions.

The key point is that you can mentor all along the road. Even when you are in an entry-level position and only beginning to learn the ropes, you can go back and tell your experiences to younger people—maybe your brother, your niece, students at a local high school or college—and share what you're learning with them.

As a Latino competing and thriving in the corporate arena, you have the honor and privilege of bringing to your corporation the value that our culture places on legacy. By offering your hand to the young people of our community who are following you up the corporate ladder, you are extending the legacy of our success into the next generation of Latino leadership.

———

The Latino community is part of a beautiful cultural mosaic that has existed for more than five hundred years. To experience the joys of success, you must never lose the connection to your heritage. For us Hispanics to make our voices resound so that America sits up and listens like never before, you must always remember who you are and where you come from.

As you make your way through your professional journey, honor those whose imprints are on the path, those who chose the road less traveled, those who cut trees, cleared rock, and smoothed the way Each of us who travels this road has a responsibility to care for it and leave it better than we found it, thus providing safe passage for those who follow. In doing so, our legacy of success will continue to flourish.

Buena suerte. . . . Buen viaje.

What good is success unless you share it?

Your greatest legacy is to repeat and multiply your success by helping someone else.

To keep the dream alive, many must pass through the doorway.

HISPANIC PROFESSIONAL ORGANIZATIONS AND HISPANIC EMPLOYEE ASSOCIATIONS

The growth in numbers of Hispanic professional organizations and Hispanic employee associations directly reflects the increase in Hispanic professionals in the workforce. These groups represent the interests of thousands of Hispanic professionals and should be looked upon as a source of information, exchange, and knowledge.

Many of these organizations have chapters in cities across the country. Some host annual conferences that attract top-notch keynote presentations, workshops, and panels addressing topics of vital importance to today's Hispanic professional. Another feature of many conferences is the inclusion of a job fair/expo where major corporations interested in the Hispanic community exhibit and recruit.

Hispanic professional organizations and employee groups provide valuable access to growth and networking opportunities. Special thanks to the National Hispanic Employees Association for their help in compiling this list.

DIRECTORY OF HISPANIC PROFESSIONAL ORGANIZATIONS

American Association of Hispanic Certified Public Accountants (AAHCPA)
19726 E. Colima Rd., Suite 270
Rowland Heights, CA 91748
(626) 965-0643 (tel)
(626) 965-0653 (fax)
http://www.aahcpa.org
Established: 1972

The American Association of Hispanic Certified Public Accountants is a national organization with the primary purpose of helping Hispanic students, accountants, and CPAs enhance their professional capabilities while expanding Hispanic representation in the nation's workforce.

Hispanic Alliance for Career Enhancement (HACE)
200 S. Michigan Ave., Suite 1210
Chicago, IL 60604
(312) 435-0498 (tel)
(312) 435-1494 (fax)
Established: 1982

The mission of the Hispanic Alliance for Career Enhancement (HACE) is to provide linkage and access for Hispanic professionals to private and public organizations, thereby strengthening the foundation for the professional and economic advancement of the Hispanic community. HACE's program focus is on enhancing career development and educational opportunities for Hispanic professionals and college students.

Hispanic National Bar Association (HNBA)
P.O. Box 66105
Washington, DC 20035
or 1700 K St., N.W., Room 1005
Washington, DC 20006
(202) 293-1507 (tel)
(202) 293-1508 (fax)
http://www.incacorp.com/hnba
E-mail: hnba@aol.com
Established: 1972

HNBA is a professional association that pursues the advancement of Hispanics in the legal profession.

Hispanic Nurses Association
10111 Northwest Park Dr.
Houston, TX 77086
(281) 591-8307 (tel)
(281) 591-8707 (fax)
http://www.hispanicnurses.org
E-mail: info@hispanicnurses.org
Established: 1995

The Hispanic Nurses Association is a nonprofit professional nursing society committed to the health-care needs of the Hispanic community and promoting the educational advancement of the Hispanic nurse. The organization is committed to the development and improvement of nursing care for all peoples, particularly Hispanics. It believes this can be accomplished by promoting leadership, professionalism, and the educational advancement of the Hispanic nurse.

Interamerican College of Physicians and Surgeons (ICPS)
1712 I St., N.W., Suite 200
Washington, DC 20006
(202) 467-4756 (tel)
(202) 467-4758 (fax)
http://www.interport.net/~icps
E-mail: webmaster@icps
Established: 1979

The Interamerican College of Physicians and Surgeons was founded in 1979 as a nonprofit national educational, charitable, and medical corporation to promote greater communication and understanding among Hispanic physicians practicing in the United States.

National Association of Hispanic Federal Executives, Inc.
   (NAHFE)
P.O. Box 469
Herndon, VA 20172
(703) 787-0291 (tel)
(703) 787-4675 (fax)
http://www.nahfe.org
Established: 1980

NAHFE's fundamental objectives were formulated to serve as an advocate for the recruitment, career development, and promotion of Hispanic Americans within the departments and agencies of the U.S. government. The association's more specific primary motivation is to increase career development opportunities for Hispanic Americans within the federal senior policymaking positions.

National Association of Hispanic Journalists (NAHJ)
1193 National Press Building
Washington, DC 20045
(202) 662-7145 (tel)
(202) 662-7144 (fax)
http://www.nahj.org
Established: 1984
NAHJ is dedicated to the recognition and professional advancement of Hispanics in the news industry. NAHJ members include working journalists, journalism students, other media-related professionals, and academic scholars.

National Association of Hispanic Public Administrators (NAHPA)
P.O. Box 142171
Coral Gables, FL 33114
(305) 596-8268 (tel)
(305) 596-8982 (fax)
Established: 1990
The National Association of Hispanic Public Administrators was organized to promote programs and activities that inspire pro-fessionalism and sound administrative practices, to help Hispanics strengthen their standing in the public sector and in their commu-nities, and to enhance and assist with career development through effective networking and information dissemination.

National Association of Hispanic Publications (NAHP)
262 National Press Building
Washington, DC 20045
(202) 662-7250 (tel)
(202) 662-7254 (fax)
Established: 1982
The mission of the NAHP is to promote Hispanic print, to pro-

vide technical assistance and information to its members, and to educate or inform on issues of concern to the readership of its members.

National Coalition of Hispanic Health and Human Services
Organizations (COSSMHO)
1501 16th St., N.W.
Washington, DC 20036
(202) 387-5000 (tel)
(202) 797-4353 (fax)
http://www.cossmho.org/
Established: 1970
    The mission of COSSMHO is to improve the health and well-being of all Hispanic communities throughout the United States. COSSMHO membership consists of frontline health and human services providers and organizations serving Hispanic communities.

National Federation of Hispanic Owned Newspapers (NFHON)
853 Broadway, Suite 811
New York, NY 10003
(212) 505-0288 (tel)
(212) 674-6861 (fax)
Established: 1968
    NFHON is a nonprofit organization comprised of Hispanic publishers from throughout the nation. Its main goal is to unite the large variety of Spanish-language newspapers in the United States to search for answers to issues affecting the Hispanic press and the communities they serve.

National Hispana Leadership Institute (NHLI)
1901 North Moore St., Suite 206
Arlington, VA 22209
(703) 527-6007 (tel)
(703) 527-6009 (fax)
E-mail: NHLI@aol.com
Established: 1987

The National Hispana Leadership Institute believes that people are the true agents of change within organizations. NHLI is a comprehensive leadership institute. Through the development of individuals, it seeks to develop communities.

National Hispanic Academy of Media Arts and Sciences, Inc.
4457 Oak St.
Pico Rivera, CA 90660
(212) 319-1373 (tel)
(212) 319-1373 (fax)
Established: 1984
The objectives of the National Hispanic Academy of Media Arts and Sciences are to establish and promote an effective networking system among the membership and the media industry targeted toward achieving improved employment conditions for Hispanics in the media; positive images of Hispanics in the media; and increased professional and educational opportunities.

National Hispanic Corporate Council (NHCC)
2323 N. Third St., Suite 101
Phoenix, AZ 85004
(602) 495-1988 (tel)
(602) 495-9085 (fax)
Established: 1985
The purpose of NHCC is twofold: (1) to serve the member Fortune 500 companies and their representatives as a principal resource for information, expertise, and counsel on selected Hispanic issues affecting corporate objectives and (2) to advocate for increased employment, leadership, and business opportunities for Hispanics in corporate America.

National Hispanic Medical Association
1700 17th St., N.W., Suite 405-2009
Washington, DC 20009
(202) 265-4297 (tel)
(202) 234-5468 (fax)
Established: 1994

The National Hispanic Medical Association represents physicians serving the Hispanic community by providing support and guidance and seeking to increase the number of Hispanic medical students in the United States.

National Society of Hispanic MBAs (NSHMBA)
P.O. Box 224747
Dallas, TX 75222-4747
(214) 428-1622 (tel)
(214) 428-2254 (fax)
http://www.nshmba.org
E-mail: nshmba@sprintmail.com
Established: 1988

The mission of NSHMBA is to foster Hispanic leadership through graduate management education and professional development in order to better society. NSHMBA, with chapters throughout the United States and in Puerto Rico, provides a forum for Latino business professionals to network, develop their professional skills, and significantly improve their long-range career progression.

Professional Hispanics In Energy (PHIE)
5275 Via Brumosa
Yorba Linda, CA 92886
(714) 777-7729 (tel)
(714) 777-7728 (fax)
Established: 1989

The purposes of PHIE are to establish a public forum to enable the Hispanic community to dialogue with the energy and environmental industries on issues of mutual concern; to create an industry forum for the exchange of information and innovative ideas regarding energy and environmental issues among Hispanics in energy and environmentally related professions; to serve as a reference source for energy and environmentally related information primarily for Spanish-speaking consumers; and to maintain a resource repository for energy and environmentally related education, training, and employment opportunities for Hispanics.

Society of Hispanic Professional Engineers (SHPE)
5400 E. Olympic Blvd., Suite 210
Los Angeles, CA 90022
(213) 725-3970 (tel)
(213) 725-0316 (fax)
http://www.shpe.net
E-mail: shpe@earthquake.net
Established: 1974
 The mission of SHPE is to promote the development of Hispanics in engineering, science, and other technical professions to achieve educational excellence, economic opportunity, and social equity.

DIRECTORY OF HISPANIC EMPLOYEE ASSOCIATIONS

National Hispanic Employee Association (NHEA)
2011 North Shoreline Blvd.
M/S 954
Mountain View, CA 94043
(650) 933-6953 (tel)
(650) 933-0878 (fax)
http://www.nhea.org/
E-mail: nhea@sgi.com
Established: 1991

It is the vision of NHEA to be the leading proponent and resource dedicated to the development and advancement of Hispanics in the corporate, public, and academic sectors. The organization's mission is to promote the upward mobility of Hispanics in the corporate, public, and academic sectors.

American Telephone and Telegraph (AT&T)
Hispanic Association of AT&T Employees (HISPA)
3200 Lake EMMA Rd., Room 2G221
Lake Mary, FL 32746
(407) 805-2104 (tel)
(407) 805-5896 (fax)

Ameritech
Ameritech Hispanic Advisory Panel
P.O. Box 295
Lake Zurich, IL 60047
(312) 727-4800 (tel)

Apple Computer
Apple Hispanic Association
1 Infinite Loop, M/S 306-2PC
Cupertino, CA 95014
(408) 974-0006

Avon Products
Avon Hispanic Network
1345 Avenue of the Americas
New York, NY 10105
(212) 282-5610 (tel)
(212) 282-6086 (fax)

Bell Atlantic
Association of Latino Employees of Bell Atlantic (ALBA)
1310 N. Court House Rd.
Arlington, VA 22201
(703) 875-8856 (tel)
(703) 528-8582 (fax)

Bell Atlantic New Jersey
Council of Action for Minority Professionals Inc. (CAMP)
P.O. Box 20310
Newark, NJ 07101
(973) 649-0526 (tel)
(201) 649-5352 (fax)

Boeing
Boeing Employee Hispanic Network (BEHN)
P.O. Box 3707
M/S 4M-58
Seattle, WA 98124
(253) 931-9401

Coors Brewing Company
Coors Hispanic Employee Network
P.O. Box 1454
Golden, CO 80401
(303) 277-5577 (tel)
(303) 277-5337 (fax)

Du Pont
Corporate Hispanic Network
Rick Otero
P.O. Box 2197
Houston, TX 77252
(281) 293-1254 (tel)
(281) 293-1650 (fax)

Hewlett Packard
La Voz
Mail Stop 46UB
19091 Pruneridge Avenue
Cupertino, CA 95014
(408) 447-0394 (tel)
(408) 447-4744 (fax)

Honeywell Inc.
Honeywell Hispanic Network (HHN)
P.O. Box 21111, Mail Stop 2K35C1
Phoenix, AZ 85036
(602) 436-6578 (tel)
(602) 436-2252 (fax)

Hughes Aircraft Company
Hughes Hispanic Network
Building E-1, M/S A114
2000 El Segundo Blvd.
El Segundo, CA 90245
(310) 616-7581 (tel)
(310) 616-3394 (fax)

Hughes Missile Systems Company
Hughes Hispanic Employee Association in Tucson
Building 811 TRLR
P.O. Box 11337
Tucson, AZ 85734
(520) 794-1029 (tel)
(520) 794-4747 (fax)

Litton Guidance & Control Systems
Litton Hispanic Employee Association (LHEA)
5500 Canoga Ave., M/S 25
Woodland Hills, CA 91367-6698
(818) 715-2705 (tel)
(818) 715-2729 (fax)

Lockheed Martin
AMISTAD
P.O. Box 179
Mail Stop DC 0092
Denver, CO 80201
(303) 977-6606 (tel)
(303) 971-2201 (fax)

Lucent Technologies
Hispanic Association of Lucent Technologies, Inc. (HISPA)
P.O. Box 30141
Gahanna, OH 43230
(614) 337-8138 (tel)
(614) 337-0824 (fax)

NCR Corporation
Hispanic Association of NCR Employees, Inc. (HISPA)
17095 Via del Campo c/o HISPA
San Diego, CA 92127
(619) 485-2852 (tel)
(619) 485-2213 (fax)

Pacific Bell
Latino Professional Association (LPA)
2600 Camino Ramon, Room 1E200E
San Ramon, CA 94583
(510) 824-8961 (tel)
(510) 866-1585 (fax)

Pacific Gas and Electric Company
Hispanic Association of PP&G
P.O. Box 56, Mailstop 104/5/30B
Avila Beach, CA 93424
(805) 545-4128 (tel)
(805) 545-4907 (fax)

Pepsico, Inc.–Frito-Lay, Inc.
Arriba
7701 Legacy Dr.
Plano, TX 75024
(972) 334-5815 (tel)
(972) 334-2695 (fax)

Polaroid Corporation
Hispanics In Polaroid (HIP)
Workforce Diversity Office
565 Technology Square, 7th Floor
Cambridge, MA 02139
(781) 386-2000 (tel)
(781) 386-3925 (fax)

Public Service Company of New Mexico
Hispanic Employee Association of Public
    Service Company of New Mexico (LLAVE)
Alvarado Square
Albuquerque, NM 87158-0600
(505) 241-2569 (tel)
(505) 241-2355 (fax)

Ryder System, Inc.
Ryder Hispanic Network
3600 N.W. 82nd Ave.
Miami, FL 33166
(305) 500-3013 (tel)
(305) 500-4739 (fax)

Silicon Graphics Computer Systems
Visionarios
M/S 160
2011 Shoreline Blvd.
Mountain View, CA 94043-1389
(650) 993-5606 (tel)
(650) 993-8549 (fax)

Southwestern Bell Corporation
Hispanic Association of Communication Employees
  (HACEMOS)
6301 Colwell, Suite 200
Irving, TX 75039
(972) 402-2300 (tel)
(972) 402-2427 (fax)

Sun Microsystems
Society of Latinos at Sun Microsystems (SOL)
901 San Antonio Rd., M/S UMIL07-120
Palo Alto, CA 94303-4900
(408) 276-3652 (tel)
(408) 934-4823 (fax)

Texas Instruments, Inc.
Hispanic Employee Initiative Forum
7839 Churchill Way, M/S 3991
Dallas, TX 75251
(972) 917-5767 (tel)
(972) 917-6132 (fax)

US West, Inc.
SOMOS: Success Oriented Members Offering Support
P.O. Box 1918
Denver, CO 80203
(303) 624-0421 (tel)
(303) 624-4927 (fax)

Xerox Corporation
Hispanic Association for Professional Advancement (HAPA)
100 Clinton Ave. S.
Rochester, NY 14644
(716) 423-3012 (fax)
http://www.hapa.org

ABOUT THE AUTHOR

JUAN ROBERTO JOB, the son of Mexican immigrants, is one of the nation's leading speakers on cultural diversity and change management. He has conducted educational and motivational workshops throughout the United States geared to Hispanic executives, students, and business leaders. He divides his time between Denver and New York.